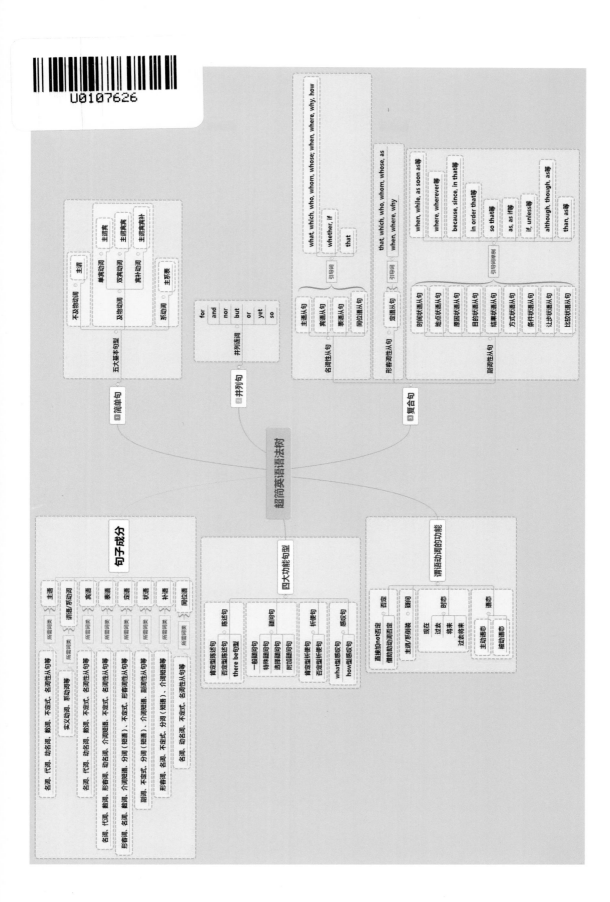

超简英语语法树

①简单句

五大基本句型

主谓
不及物动词
主谓宾
单宾动词
及物动词
双宾动词 主谓双宾
主谓宾宾补
宾补动词
主系表
系动词

②并列句

并列连词
for
and
nor
but
or
yet
so

③复合句

名词性从句
主语从句
宾语从句
表语从句
同位语从句

引导词
what, which, who, whom, whose; when, why, how
whether, if
that

形容词性从句
定语从句

引导词
that, which, who, whom, whose, as
when, where, why

副词性从句
时间状语从句
地点状语从句
原因状语从句
目的状语从句
结果状语从句
方式状语从句
条件状语从句
让步状语从句
比较状语从句

引导词
when, while, as soon as等
where, wherever等
because, since, in that等
in order that等
so that等
as, as if等
if, unless等
although, though, as等
than, as等

句子成分

主语
谓语/系动词
实义动词
宾语
表语
定语
状语
补语
同位语

所属词类
名词、代词、动名词、数词、不定式、名词性从句等
实义动词、系动词
名词、代词、动名词、数词、不定式、名词性从句等
名词、代词、数词、形容词、不定式、名词性从句等
形容词、数词、介词短语、分词（短语）、不定式、形容词性从句等
副词、不定式、名词、介词短语、分词（短语）、介词短语等
形容词、名词、不定式、分词（短语）、介词短语等
名词、动名词、不定式、名词性从句等

四大功能句型

陈述句
肯定型陈述句
否定型陈述句
there be句型

疑问句
一般疑问句
特殊疑问句
选择疑问句
附加疑问句

祈使句
肯定型祈使句
否定型祈使句

感叹句
what型感叹句
how型感叹句

谓语动词的功能

否定
直接加not否定
借助助动词否定

疑问
主谓/系倒装

时态
现在
过去
将来
过去将来

语态
主动语态
被动语态

超简
英语语法

左高超 主编

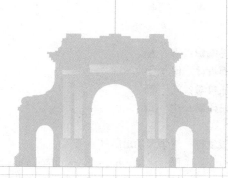

清华大学出版社
北京

内容简介

本书适用于想要掌握英语句子构成的读者。本书紧紧围绕英语句子的构成展开讲解，化繁为简，揭示英语句子的底层逻辑，旨在帮助读者构建英语语法知识体系，彻悟英语句型。全书分为 10 章。第 1 章讲解英语的基本句型。第 2 章讲解英语句子的成分和各类词性的基本对应关系。第 3 章讲解谓语动词的常见功能。第 4 章讲解陈述句、疑问句、祈使句和感叹句。第 5 章讲解三大结构句型。第 6 章讲解名词性从句的构成方法。第 7 章讲解定语从句的构成方法。第 8 章讲解状语从句的构成方法。第 9 章讲解省略与强调等。第 10 章是综合实践，本章选取各类英语考试历年真题中的句子作为材料，引导读者独立分析英语句型，以检测学习效果。

本书配有由左高超老师主讲的英语语法核心知识导学视频，读者可扫描书中二维码，获取精品课程。

图书在版编目（CIP）数据

超简英语语法 / 左高超主编. —北京：清华大学出版社，2024.4
ISBN 978-7-302-65978-5

Ⅰ.①超…　Ⅱ.①左…　Ⅲ.①英语－语法－自学参考资料　Ⅳ.① H314

中国国家版本馆CIP数据核字（2024）第068079号

责任编辑：雷　桢
封面设计：傅瑞学
责任校对：刘　静
责任印制：沈　露

出版发行：清华大学出版社
　　　　　网　　　址：https://www.tup.com.cn，https://www.wqxuetang.com
　　　　　地　　　址：北京清华大学学研大厦A座　　　　邮　　编：100084
　　　　　社 总 机：010-83470000　　　　　　　　　　邮　　购：010-62786544
　　　　　投稿与读者服务：010-62776969，c-service@tup.tsinghua.edu.cn
　　　　　质量反馈：010-62772015，zhiliang@tup.tsinghua.edu.cn
印 装 者：三河市人民印务有限公司
经　　销：全国新华书店
开　　本：185mm×260mm　　印　　张：7.75　插页：1　　字　　数：174 千字
版　　次：2024年4月第1版　　　　　　　　　　　　　印　　次：2024年4月第1次印刷
定　　价：39.00元

产品编号：092368–01

编　委　会

本书适用于初级、中级水平的英语学习者。

本书的特色如下。

第一，聚焦句子构成，直击学习痛点

很多人背了很多单词，却看不懂句子、动不了笔、开不了口，其背后的原因就是不理解句子的构成。本书针对这个问题，系统讲解英语各类句型，帮助读者迅速掌握英语句子构成的方法，为其有效地使用英语打下坚实的基础。

第二，讲解由浅入深，方法实用有效

本书首先从最简单的五大句型和七大成分开始讲解，并把各个成分和词性的匹配关系对应清楚；然后逐步深入地讲解英语各种句型的构成，让句子结构不再晦涩难懂；最后对考试真题中的句子进行分析，让所学有所用。

第三，抛开烦琐细节，宏观把握句型

各种烦琐的细节会让人对英语语法的学习望而生畏。所以本书抛开大量烦琐的英语语法细节，将搭建句型作为重中之重。这样有助于读者宏观把握句型，而不至于迷失在各类语法细节当中。

第四，讲解结合练习，配套视频辅助

为了学习效果，本书特在每章之后设置知识应用部分，深化学习效果。练习题目均来自各类考试真题。

本书配有由左高超老师主讲的英语语法核心知识导学视频，读者可扫描书中二维码，获取英语语法精品课程。

欢迎广大读者与左高超老师交流互动。

微信公众号：超简英语语法

编　者

2024 年 2 月

目　录

《超简英语语法》
配套视频课程

英语的基本句型

学英语离不开句型。英语中长难句很多，但通常是在基本句型的基础上逐步添加各种成分才变得长而难的。所以想要弄懂英语句子，尤其是各类复杂句子，就要先了解英语句子的基本构成方法。

按照比较常见的分类方法，英语中共有五种基本句型（除少量特殊句型外），如表 1-1 所示。

表 1-1　五种基本句型

句　型	谓语动词类型	例　句
主 + 谓	不及物动词	Michael smiles.
主 + 谓 + 宾	单宾动词	English helped me.
主 + 谓 + 宾 + 宾	双宾动词	My mother made me a cake.
主 + 谓 + 宾 + 宾补	宾补动词	A teacher told me to come.
主 + 系 + 表	系动词	The boy is handsome.

由表 1-1 可知，决定这五种基本句型的因素是谓语动词。从构成基本句型的角度分类，谓语动词分为三大类：不及物动词、及物动词（又分为单宾动词、双宾动词和宾补动词）和系动词。这些动词类型决定了英语中的五种基本句型。需要说明的是，本章所谈的是简单句，所举的例子也尽量以简单句为主（有时出现从句仅仅是为了说明情况，更详细的从句内容会在各从句章节探讨）。

1.1　"主 + 谓"句型

"主 + 谓"句型是由不及物动词充当谓语的句子结构。由于不及物动词不需要宾语来补充，所以形成的句子仅有主语和谓语。

Michael smiles.

迈克尔面露微笑。

He arrived.

他到了。

The sun shines.

太阳照耀。

有一些动词短语可以充当不及物动词使用。

The plane takes off at 9 o' clock.

飞机九点起飞。

We should never give in.

我们绝不应该屈服。

Don' t give up.

不要自暴自弃。

需要说明的是，定语和状语通常属于非必要成分，所以句子中的定语或状语并不影响句子结构的类型。例如，下面两个句子仍然属于"主＋谓"句型。

She turned to me for help.

她向我求助。

The little girl' s mouth watered for chocolate.

这个小女孩想吃巧克力，流了口水。

但英语中有些动词的状语是必不可少的（在某个特定含义下）。

The path leads to a splendid hall.

这条路通往一个富丽堂皇的大厅。

动词 lead 在作不及物动词表示"通往"含义时，后面的状语必不可少。正因为这类状语的存在，有人在五大基本句型之外又加了另一个句型（"主＋谓＋状"句型），但由于其数量较少，所以我们仅仅把它看成例外情况，而不单列成一种句型。

1.2 "主＋谓＋宾"句型

"主＋谓＋宾"句型是由单宾动词充当谓语的句子结构。单宾动词又称单一宾语及物动词（mono-transitive verb），它需要一个宾语来补充其含义。

I love English.

我爱英语。

English can help us.

英语能够帮助我们。

有些不及物动词加上相应的介词可以作为单宾动词使用。

He looks at me.

他看着我。

We often talk about you.

我们常常谈起你。

有些动词短语可以整体当作单宾动词使用。

He got rid of the mice in his kitchen.

他除掉了厨房里的老鼠。

I am looking forward to the holiday.

我正盼望着假期。

Don't give up hope.

别放弃希望。

有些动词既可以用作不及物动词，也可以用作及物动词（用法不同，含义可能也有所不同）。

Birds fly in the sky.（不及物动词）

鸟在天空中飞翔。

I like flying kites.（及物动词）

我喜欢放风筝。

He didn't speak to me.（不及物动词）

他没和我说话。

Can you speak English?（及物动词）

你能说英语吗？

My face burned.（不及物动词）

我的脸发烫。

He burned the books.（及物动词）

他把这些书烧了。

My parents and I used to live in Beijing.（不及物动词）

我和我父母以前住在北京。

Grown-ups should leave their parents and live their own lives.（及物动词）

成年人应该离开父母过自己的生活。

1.3 "主 + 谓 + 宾 + 宾"句型

"主 + 谓 + 宾 + 宾"句型是由双宾动词充当谓语的句子结构。双宾动词又称双宾语及物动词（ditransitive verb），这类动词需要两个宾语。

从位置上讲，间接宾语通常位于直接宾语前。

Jack told me an interesting story.

杰克给我讲了一个有趣的故事。

Jack gave Jane a book.

杰克给了简一本书。

My mother made me a cake.

我的母亲给我做了一个蛋糕。

间接宾语和直接宾语的位置通常可以互换，但往往需要介词辅助，常见的介词有 to（通常表示动作的朝向，即给谁）和 for（通常表示动作的目的，即为谁而做）。

Jack told an interesting story to me.

杰克给我讲了一个有趣的故事。

Jack gave a book to Jane.

杰克给了简一本书。

My mother made a cake for me.

我的母亲为我做了一个蛋糕。

He bought a dress for his girlfriend.

他为他女朋友买了一件裙子。

有些动词的双宾语需要借助相应的介词构成，这些介词通常为 of, about, to, with, for 等。

My parents expect too much of me.

我父母对我期待太高。

A gang of criminals robbed the old lady of all her money.

一群罪犯抢走了这个老妇人所有的钱。

Don't forget to remind me of tomorrow's meeting.

不要忘了提醒我明天的会议。

Could you please tell me about your experiences in the Middle East?

你能给我讲讲你在中东的经历吗？

The power plant supplies electricity to the town.

这家电厂给这个镇提供电力。

Parents should provide their children with food and education.

父母应该给孩子提供食物和教育。

Parents should provide food and education for their children.

父母应该给孩子提供食物和教育。

1.4 "主+谓+宾+宾补"句型

"主+谓+宾+宾补"句型是由宾补动词充当谓语的句子结构。宾补动词又称复合及物动词（complex transitive verb），这类动词的宾语后需要一个宾语补足语。

I will make you happy.
我会让你幸福的。
They want me to visit the museum.
他们想让我参观博物馆。

有许多宾补动词并不仅仅作为专门的宾补动词，它们还可能同时属于其他类别。

I made a mistake.（单宾动词）
我犯了一个错误。
I made her a cake.（双宾动词）
我给她做了一个蛋糕。
I made her happy.（宾补动词）
我让她很开心。
Nancy got home very late last night.（不及物动词）
南希昨天晚上到家特别晚。
I got good marks for English and maths.（单宾动词）
我英语和数学都考了很高的分数。
That behavior got him a bad reputation.（双宾动词）
那个行为给他带来了坏名声。
Who can get him to stay for the night?（宾补动词）
谁能让他留下来过夜？
It is getting cold.（系动词）
天气正在变冷。

1.5　"主 + 系 + 表" 句型

"主 + 系 + 表" 句型是含有系动词的句子结构。系动词又称连系动词（linking verb），这类动词后面通常跟一个表语来表明主语的情况（身份或状态等）。

Jack is a teacher.
杰克是一位老师。
Jack is happy.
杰克很幸福。
The fish smells bad.
这条鱼闻起来臭了。
Dawn seemed annoyed.
道恩似乎很恼火。

He appeared unaware of the matter.

他好像没意识到这件事。

The public went wild.

公众都疯狂了。

The dream has finally come true.

这个梦想终于成真了。

知 识 应 用

请指出下列句子分别属于五种基本句型中的哪一种。

1. Children need time to stand and stare.

2. Brian was a funny student.

3. He loved watching comedies best.

4. He had never acted on stage before.

5. Brian did a great job at the talent show.

6. Everyone loved his performance.

7. His teachers and friends were proud of him.

8. He confidently continued to work towards his goal.

9. Luckily, most people encouraged him.

10. His comedies made his fans feel good.

英语句子的成分

通常可以把句子成分分为主语、谓语、宾语、定语、状语、补语和同位语七种，但当句子属于"主＋系＋表"句型时，谓语和宾语的位置分别为系动词和表语，所以本章将分别讨论这九种成分。

2.1 ▶ 主语

从五种基本句型可以看出，主语属于句子的必要成分，除特殊情况外（如祈使句中省略主语等），主语是不可缺少的。充当主语成分的词（短语或从句）包括名词、代（名）词、动名词、名词化的形容词、名词性从句、数词和动词不定式等。

1. 名词作主语

The Beijing-Hangzhou Grand Canal is the longest canal in the world and an invaluable cultural heritage.

京杭大运河是世界上最长的人工运河，也是十分宝贵的文化遗产。

The book has a good influence on young people.

这本书对年轻人有好的影响。

Dictionaries are of great use to language learners.

词典对语言学习者很有用。

2. 代（名）词作主语

What made you think that way?

是什么让你那么想的？

I can't help you.

我不能帮助你。

Something happened.

发生了一件事。

3. 动名词（短语）作主语

Swimming is my favorite sport.
游泳是我最喜欢的运动。

充当主语的动名词前可使用所有格形式或形容词性物主代词作为其逻辑主语。

Mary's coming surprised me.
玛丽的到来让我很吃惊。
His being sick caused the meeting to be cancelled.
他生病导致会议被取消了。

4. 名词化的形容词作主语

Generally speaking, the young are less conservative than the old.
总的来说，年轻人没有老年人那么保守。
The rich should help the poor.
富人应该帮助穷人。

5. 名词性从句作主语

What he said was wrong.
他说的是错的。
Whether this kind of pesticide is harmful to plants still puzzles many scientists.
这种杀虫剂是否对植物有害仍然困扰着很多科学家。
Who will take this task has not been decided yet.
谁来做这个工作还没有确定下来。

6. 数词作主语

One plus one equals two.
一加一等于二。
Thirty divided by six gives five.
三十除以六等于五。
Eight is a multiple of four.
八是四的倍数。

7. 动词不定式作主语

To understand that is hard.
理解起来很难。
To gossip about others is not right.
说别人闲话是不对的。

> ✒️ **注意：**
>
> 1. 动词不定式 to do 作主语常常被置于句尾，句首要用 it 作为形式主语。
>
> It is encouraging to learn that the employees in this company enjoy their work.
>
> 令人鼓舞的是，这家公司的员工很喜欢他们的工作。
>
> It is important to learn English grammar.
>
> 学习英语语法是很重要的。
>
> 2. 表示具体某个人的行为，也可以给 to do 不定式加上逻辑主语。
>
> For such a little child to do this difficult job is just impossible.
>
> 这么小的孩子做这么困难的工作是不可能的。

8. it 作形式主语

当不定式或从句等充当的主语后置时，句首要用 it 作为形式主语。

It is important for scientific workers to know foreign languages.

对科技工作者来说，懂外语很重要。

It is easy to use a computer.

使用计算机很简单。

It is essential that you make the right decisions.

重要的是你要做出正确的决定。

2.2 谓语

谓语直接决定了英语的基本句型，而且它参与的语法功能非常多，包括主谓一致、时态、否定、被动语态、疑问、倒装和虚拟语气等。虽然谓语要承担的功能很多，但是它自身要求的词性却相对单一，即只有动词才能作谓语（情态动词和助动词不能独立作谓语）。

He smiles.

他微笑。

I like English.

我喜欢英语。

He told me an interesting story.

他给我讲了一个有趣的故事。

He can speak seven foreign languages.

他能说七门外语。

We have already learned many idioms.

我们已经学了很多习语。

I do not know anything about it.

我对这件事一无所知。

John was punished by his father.

约翰被他父亲惩罚了。

He is smiling.

他在微笑。

The President is to visit China this weekend.

总统计划本周末访华。

由于谓语动词功能多且复杂，所以将在第 3 章中单独讨论谓语的常见用法。

2.3 ▶ 系动词

在所有系动词中，be 动词是最重要也是最常见的。除 be 动词之外，常用系动词还可以分为三大类，即现状类系动词（感觉动词 smell, sound, taste, look 等，以及表象动词 appear, seem 等）、保持类系动词（stay, remain 等）和结果类系动词（become, come, get, go, prove, turn 等）。

1. be 动词

English is an international language.

英语是一门国际性语言。

Language study is interesting and challenging.

语言学习有趣又有挑战。

This idea is of no importance.

这个想法不重要。

2. 现状类系动词

The drink tastes sour.

这个饮品尝起来是酸的。

You appear rather sad.

你似乎很不开心。

She seems very happy with the new job.

她似乎对这份新工作很满意。

3. 保持类系动词

The weather will stay fine for three days.

天气会持续晴朗三天。

She remained silent all night.

她整晚都沉默不语。

4. 结果类系动词

The plan has proved a great success.
这项计划结果非常成功。
Leaves turn brown in autumn.
树叶在秋天变黄。

2.4 宾语

宾语分为直接宾语和间接宾语（介词宾语等不包含在内）。和主语类似，宾语所需要的通常是名词性的词（短语或从句），包括名词、代（名）词、动名词、名词化的形容词、名词性从句、数词和不定式等。

1. 名词作宾语

I like English.
我喜欢英语。
Recent years have witnessed great changes.
近些年见证了巨大的变化。
The county suffered severe job losses.
该县遭受了严重的失业问题。

2. 代（名）词作宾语

I can't help him.
我不能帮助他。
They gave me some chocolate.
他们给了我一些巧克力。
You should take good care of yourself.
你应该照顾好你自己。

3. 动名词作宾语

Jane enjoys reading these books very much.
简非常喜欢读这些书。

充当宾语的动名词前可使用所有格形式或人称代词的宾格作为其逻辑主语。

I don't like his coming so often.
我不喜欢他老来。
Do you mind me opening the door?
你介意我开门吗？

4. 名词化的形容词作宾语

We should help the old.
我们应该帮助老年人。

She took care of the wounded.
她照顾了伤员。

5. 名词性从句作宾语

She said that she was satisfied.
她说她很满意。

I only believe what I see.
我只相信我看到的。

6. 数词作宾语

Three plus two equals five.
三加二等于五。

Eight and six make fourteen.
八加六等于十四。

7. 不定式作宾语

I decide to master English.
我决定要掌握英语。

The girl wants to play in the yard.
这个女孩想在院子里玩。

I will remember to tell you the story.
我会记得给你讲这个故事。

有些动词在后跟不定式或动名词作宾语时，含义有所区别。

I remember telling you the story.
我记得给你讲过这个故事。

I will remember to tell you the story.
我会记得给你讲这个故事。

有些动词在后跟不定式或动名词作宾语时，含义是基本一致的（或者仅有细微的差别）。

I started to learn English last year.
我去年开始学习英语。

I started learning English last year.

我去年开始学习英语。

I like playing football.

我喜欢踢足球。

I like to play football.

我喜欢踢足球。

虽然在这种情况下用不定式或动名词的语义差别很小，但在一定语境下这种差别还是可以感受到的，不定式往往表示未做而要做的含义，而动名词往往表示反复或者进行的含义。这个区别可以通过加入一些条件来体现。

I like to play football this afternoon.

我今天下午想去踢足球。

He started to talk and was interrupted almost immediately.

他刚一开口说话，就立刻被打断了。

Once he started talking, he was unwilling to stop.

一旦他开口说话，他就不愿意停下来。

I hate to bother you, but I need your help desperately now.

我真不想打扰你，但我现在真的非常需要你的帮助。

I really hate bothering you all the time.

我真不喜欢一直打扰你。

8. it 作形式宾语

English makes it possible for us to communicate with foreigners.

英语使我们和外国人交流成为可能。

You may find it difficult to get along with him.

你可能会发现和他相处很难。

2.5　表语

不同的系动词对所跟表语的要求不尽相同。其中 be 动词后跟的表语类别是最多的，而有些系动词对后跟的表语限制很严格。下面仅从表语的角度举出部分例子。

1. 名词作表语

That seems a good idea.

那似乎是个很好的主意。

She sounds just the person we need.

听起来她正是我们需要的人。

2. 代（名）词作表语

He is not himself today.
他今天不在状态。
The book is hers.
这本书是她的。

3. 数词作表语

Eight and six are fourteen.
八加六等于十四。
Eight plus six is fourteen.
八加六等于十四。

4. 形容词作表语

This is very important.
这事非常重要。
She turned pale with fright.
她害怕得脸都发白了。
The house stands empty.
这所房子空空如也。

5. 动名词作表语

Seeing is believing.
眼见为实。
Her job is washing clothes.
她的工作是洗衣服。

6. 介词短语作表语

Tony is in good health.
托尼健康状态不错。
Jane was out of breath.
简上气不接下气。

7. 不定式作表语

His aim is to become president.
他的目标是成为总统。
You seem to be very nervous.
你好像很紧张。

8. 名词性从句作表语

My suggestion is that we wait a day or two.
我的建议是我们等上一两天。
It seemed that he was determined to oppose her.
他似乎决心要反对她。

9. 副词（从句）作表语
少量副词或副词性从句可以作表语。

The light is on.
灯亮着。
He will be here next week.
他下周会在这里。
It is because I need your help desperately.
这是因为我非常需要你的帮助。

2.6 宾语补足语

为了和本章讲述的基本句型对应，这里介绍宾语补足语。宾语补足语往往指一种结果（谓语动词作用于宾语而产生的结果，宾语补足语和宾语具有逻辑上的主谓关系）。

1. 形容词作宾语补足语

The news made Jack resentful.
这条新闻让杰克愤愤不平。
He always makes me happy.
他总是让我开心。

2. 名词（短语）作宾语补足语

I made the room my study.
我把这个房间变成了我的书房。
They named their child Jack.
他们给孩子起名为杰克。

3. 副词作宾语补足语
少量副词可以作宾语补足语。

They kept their dog indoors.
他们把他们的狗关在室内。
Let the dog out.
让这条狗出去。

4. 介词短语作宾语补足语

We regard you as our best friend.
我们把你看成我们最好的朋友。
Maggie talked her father into buying a car for her.
玛姬劝说她父亲给她买了一辆车。

5. 不定式作宾语补足语

Life forced him to travel from place to place.
生活迫使他四处奔波。
Jackie told me to come here to see him.
杰克告诉我来这里见他。

不定式作主语补足语时，其逻辑主语为句子里的主语。

I was told to deliver a package to the office.
我被告知要送一个包裹到办公室。

不定式作宾语补语时有省略不定式符号 to 的现象，这种现象主要取决于谓语动词。

Don't make me do that.
不要强迫我做那件事。
My mother always makes me go to bed early.
我的妈妈总是让我早睡觉。

6. 分词作宾语补足语

To get things done, we must make our voices heard.
为了把事情做好，我们必须让我们的声音被听到。
You almost got yourself killed.
你差点害了你自己。
I saw my face reflected in the water.
我看到我的脸被倒映在水中。
We are sorry for keeping you waiting.
我们很抱歉让你久等了。
I heard him singing a song.
我听到他在唱一首歌。

在一些被动语态的句子中，分词的逻辑主语是句子的主语，因此分词充当的是主语补足语。

He was heard singing a song.

他被听到在唱一首歌。

We were kept waiting at the gate.

我们只得在门口等待。

2.7　状语

状语虽然通常不是句子的必要成分，但它的作用非常强大。副词、介词短语、分词（短语）、不定式和副词性从句等都能在句子中作状语。

从修饰功能上讲，状语分为起修饰作用的状语、起评论作用的状语和起连接作用的状语。

起修饰作用的状语主要包括时间、地点、方式、原因、结果、让步、条件、比较和目的等，在句子里主要起修饰其他成分的作用。

He ran away quickly.

他飞快地跑走了。

Jane dances on the table.

简在桌子上跳舞。

I went there to see him.

我去那里看他。

起评论作用的状语并不对句子里的某个成分进行修饰，它往往修饰整个句子，通常属于说话人对句子内容的评论。

Fortunately, ancient men made tools of stone.

幸运的是，古人制作了石头工具。

With all due respect, I think you should be more generous to these people.

恕我直言，我认为你应该对这些人更慷慨一些。

Generally speaking, English grammar is not too difficult.

总的来说，英语的语法不太难。

To be honest, this article is far from being satisfactory.

说实话，这篇文章远远不能令人满意。

起连接作用的状语主要用于表示两个意义单位之间的关系。

The dress is expensive. However, it fits me perfectly.

这件裙子很贵，然而它却非常合我的身。

It is too expensive. Moreover, I don't like the style.

它是很贵，而且我不喜欢这个风格。

Practice enough before you take the test. Otherwise, you will receive a low mark.

在考试前你要做足够的练习，否则你会考低分的。

1. 副词作状语

Today, we are going to have a test.
今天我们要举行考试。

Slowly but surely, the soldiers moved forward.
士兵们缓慢但坚定地向前移动。

Mary and her parents recently moved to New York.
玛丽和她的父母最近搬到了纽约。

2. 介词短语作状语

I met him in the park.
我在公园见到了他。

Only by practice can we learn English well.
只有通过练习，我们才能学好英语。

In short, the groundless opinion should not be supported.
总之，这个没有根据的观点不应该被支持。

3. 分词（短语）作状语
分词在作状语时，往往要求其逻辑主语为句子的主语。

Walking in the street, I met Tom.
在街上散步时，我遇到了汤姆。

Born and raised in Havana, the writer drew invaluable inspiration from the city.
在哈瓦那出生并长大，这位作家从这个城市获得宝贵的灵感。

Punished by his manager, the young man felt disappointed at his job.
这个年轻人被经理惩罚了，他对工作感觉到失望。

Praised by his neighbors for his willingness to help, the boy has become the pride of his parents.

这个男孩被邻居表扬乐于助人，他成为他父母的骄傲。

Asked about his private life, the actor kept silent.
被问到私生活，这位演员一言不发。

一些表示评论的分词短语不要求逻辑主语为句子的主语。

Generally speaking, English is not difficult.
总的来说，英语不难。

Judging from his appearance, the little boy must be from a wealthy family.
从外表看，这个小男孩一定来自一个富裕家庭。

4. 不定式作状语
不定式在作状语时，往往要求其逻辑主语为句子的主语。

To get there on time, we took the fastest vehicle.

为了准时到达那里，我们坐了最快的车。

I learn English to communicate with other people.

我学英语是为了跟其他人交流。

I went to London to see Mary.

我去伦敦见玛丽。

I arrived there, only to find an empty house.

我到了那里，却只发现了一栋空房子。

一些表示评论的不定式作状语时，不要求逻辑主语为句子的主语。

To be frank, you have little chance of passing the exam.

坦白讲，你通过考试的可能性很小。

5. 副词性从句作状语

If you want to go, you can go now.

如果你想走，现在可以走了。

Although the task is difficult, I can conquer it with hard work.

尽管任务很难，我可以通过努力攻克它。

He is watching TV while I am doing my homework.

我在做家庭作业时，他在看电视。

2.8　定语

定语的主要作用是修饰或限定名词或代词等，表示其性质或特征。定语分为前置定语和后置定语，前置定语放在被修饰对象的前面，后置定语则放在被修饰对象的后面。

Have you met his handsome father?

你见过他帅气的父亲吗？

The students wearing school uniforms today will receive gifts.

今天穿校服的学生将会得到礼物。

形容词、名词、动名词、数词（以及一些表达数量的短语）、分词（短语）、不定式、介词短语、形容词性从句和部分副词等都可以在句子中作定语。

1. 形容词作定语

Jack is a cute boy.

杰克是一个可爱的男孩。

You did a perfect job.

你工作做得很完美。

The three-year-old boy shows great interest in the toy duck.
这个三岁的小男孩对这个玩具鸭子表现出了很大的兴趣。
We want to invite you to share up-to-date information in this field.
我们想邀请你分享这个领域的最新信息。

表语形容词作定语时，通常置于被修饰名词之后。

He says that he is the happiest man alive.
他说他是世上最幸福的人。
The employees present were all excited to learn the news.
在场的员工们听到这个消息都很激动。

2. 名词作定语

The car stopped at the school gate.
小汽车在学校门口停下了。
I need to find a car park.
我需要找一个停车场。
The man in the car felt nervous when a customs inspector approached.
当海关检察官靠近时，车里的男人感觉很紧张。
Is there a sporting goods store near here?
这附近有体育用品商店吗？

man 和 woman 作定语表示性别，如果被修饰的名词是复数，则它们也需要使用复数形式。

The women teachers in the school seem more patient with their students.
这个学校的女教师们似乎对学生更耐心一些。
I want a man doctor to perform the physical examination.
我想让一位男医生来做身体检查。

名词作定语与其派生形容词作定语时含义不同。

I heard a success story.
我听了一个关于成功的故事。
I heard a successful story.
我听了一个很成功的故事。
He is a health expert.
他是一名健康方面的专家。
He is a healthy expert.
他是一个很健康的专家。

3. 动名词作定语

动名词作定语，通常表示被修饰名词的功能、用途等，置于被修饰的名词之前。

I have a sleeping bag.
我有一个睡袋。

He is in the reading room.
他在阅览室。

There is a big swimming pool in the yard.
院子里有一个很大的游泳池。

4. 数词（以及一些表达数量的短语）作定语

Five students have been chosen to perform the experiment.
五名学生被选择来做这项实验。

One hundred US dollars is not enough.
一百美元不够。

I have a lot of friends.
我有很多朋友。

Recent years have witnessed an increasing number of inventions.
近些年有了越来越多的发明。

5. 分词（短语）作定语

The boy standing at the gate is my brother.
站在门口的那个男孩是我的哥哥。

The problem being discussed at the meeting is very important.
会上正在谈论的问题非常重要。

The report written by the team was praised by the committee.
这个小组写的报告受到了委员会的赞扬。

The boy punished by his father is Tom.
那个被父亲惩罚的男孩是汤姆。

6. 不定式作定语

I have nothing to say.
我没什么要说的。

Our monitor is always the first to come.
我们的班长总是第一个来。

7. 介词短语作定语

People in China are all very friendly.

中国民众都非常友好。

I ate the apple on the table.

我吃了桌子上的苹果。

A boy of seventeen described his dream university to me.

一个十七岁的男孩给我描述了他梦想中的大学。

8. 形容词性从句作定语

I enjoy reading the book that I bought yesterday.

我喜欢读我昨天买的那本书。

Her mother, who is a health specialist, will come to see her very soon.

她的妈妈是一位健康专家，很快要来看望她。

I still remember the day on which I joined the army.

我仍然记得我参军的那一天。

9. 部分副词作定语

People there were very friendly to me.

那里的人对我都非常友好。

The meeting yesterday was very successful.

昨天的会议很成功。

You can find the details in the sentence below.

你可以在下面的句子里找到细节。

I remember almost nothing about the day.

我对那一天的事几乎什么都不记得了。

Nearly everybody accepts this idea.

几乎每个人都接受这个主意。

2.9 同位语

基本来讲，同位关系是名词间的一种关系，同位语通常是对一个名词成分的解释或说明，以达到表达更清晰或更详细的目的。

President Lee is going to visit our school.

李总统准备访问我们学校。

Mr. Smith, a professor from Maryland University, will lecture on English learning.

史密斯先生，一名来自马里兰大学的教授，将要做英语学习方面的演讲。

A gifted story-teller, Linda is an expert at describing people and places.

琳达是一个在讲故事方面很有天赋的人，精通对人物和地点的描述。

除解释或说明名词外，同位语还可以对句子进行解释或说明。

Fewer and fewer students show interest in English, a situation that worries the educator.
越来越少的学生表现出对英语的兴趣，这个情况让这位教育家很担心。

承担同位语成分的词性通常包括名词、动名词、不定式和名词性从句等。

1. 名词和动名词（短语）作同位语

Jason Box, an associate professor of geology, believes that another factor should not be ignored.
地理学副教授杰森·伯克斯相信另一个因素不应该被忽略。
Greek yogurt—a form of cultured yogurt—has grown enormously in popularity.
希腊酸奶 —— 一种经过培养的酸奶—— 变得大受欢迎。
For her wedding, the actress is going to spend one million US dollars, that is, 6,500,400 yuan.
这位女演员为了婚礼准备花 100 万美元（约合 650.04 万元人民币）。
His goal, mastering English, is understandable.
他的目标是掌握英语，这是可以理解的。
His suggestion, attacking at night, has been accepted.
他的夜攻建议被采纳了。

2. 不定式短语作同位语

My method for doing this, to find a new manager, has been presented to the committee.
我做这件事的方法是找一个新经理，这一方法已经提交给委员会了。
The question whether to help him has yet to be discussed.
是否要帮他，这一问题还需要讨论。
His purpose, to impress his friends by standing on his head, is understandable.
他想通过倒立来给朋友留下深刻印象，这一目的是可以理解的。

3. 名词性从句作同位语

The fact that China is a large country is true.
中国是一个大国的事实是真的。
We are surprised at the news that the young actor wanted to retire.
听到这个年轻演员想退休的消息，我们都很吃惊。
The scientists hold a view that the Sun will die some day.
这些科学家们有一个观点，就是太阳将会在某一天灭亡。

知识应用

请指出下列句子里画线部分的词性和所充当的句子成分。

1. <u>Humans</u> produce more than 300 million tons of <u>plastic</u> every year.

2. Almost half of that <u>winds up</u> in landfills, and up to 12 million tons pollute the oceans.

3. So far there is no <u>effective</u> way to get rid of it.

4. The worms <u>of the greater wax moth</u> can break down polyethylene.

5. The team left 100 wax worms on a commercial polyethylene <u>shopping</u> bag for 12 hours, and the worms consumed and broke down about 92 milligrams, or almost 3% of it.

6. The worms' <u>chewing</u> alone was not responsible for the polyethylene breakdown.

7. Their <u>findings</u> were published in Current Biology in 2017.

8. The worms' ability <u>to break down their everyday food</u>—beeswax—also allows them to break down plastic.

9. The wax worm evolved a method or system <u>to break this bond</u>.

10. The next step will be <u>to identify the cause of the breakdown</u>.

谓 语 动 词

　　谓语动词作为重要的句子成分，其功能包括主谓一致、时态、语态、否定、倒装和虚拟语气等。本章主要从主谓一致、时态、被动语态和否定等方面讲解谓语动词的主要功能，倒装和虚拟语气会在本书后面章节里的相关部分详细讲解。

3.1　主谓一致

　　主谓一致是指谓语和主语在形式上要保持数的一致，如当主语是第三人称单数时，谓语动词要用相应的单数形式。

He watches TV every day.
他每天看电视。

　　主谓一致原则还要注意时态及情态动词等因素。动词的第三人称单数形式通常只体现在现在时态，在过去时态中一般没有第三人称单数形式（be 动词及被动语态的谓语动词的过去式除外）。

He watched TV.
他看了电视。
They watched TV.
他们看了电视。

情态动词没有第三人称单数形式。

He can speak several foreign languages.
他能讲好几门外语。
They can speak several foreign languages.
他们能讲好几门外语。

3.1.1 第三人称单数

动词第三人称单数形式的规则变化和名词复数的变化基本一致。下面通过表 3-1 呈现三个基本动词（be, have, do）和各人称的对应情况。

表 3-1　谓语动词形式与主语人称的对应关系示例

动词	第一人称单数	第二人称单数	第三人称单数	第一人称复数	第二人称复数	第三人称复数
be	am	are	is	are	are	are
have	have	have	has	have	have	have
do	do	do	does	do	do	do

请参考下面的例子。

Time flies.
时光飞逝。
Thompson seldom goes out.
汤普森很少出去。
He is doing his homework.
他正在做他的家庭作业。
He has finished his homework.
他已经完成了他的家庭作业。

3.1.2 谓语单复数的判断方法

1. 主语属于单数的情况

主语是单数名词或代词、不可数名词、动名词、不定式和名词性从句等时，谓语通常用单数。

Water is necessary for life.
水是生命所必不可少的。
Something unusual catches my attention.
有件不同寻常的事吸引了我的注意。
Seeing is believing.
眼见为实。
To learn English is necessary.
学英语是必要的。
How he escaped was a mystery.
他如何逃跑的是一个谜。

2. 主语属于复数的情况

当主语是复数名词时，谓语通常用复数。

My friends are coming to my house to celebrate my birthday.
我的朋友们准备来我家给我庆祝生日。
A lot of students show great interest in this subject.
很多学生都对这门课很感兴趣。
People change their names when they surf the Internet to protect their privacy.
为了保护自己的隐私，人们在网上冲浪时改名字。
The police are searching for the criminal.
警察正在追捕罪犯。

3. 中心词原则

名词短语作主语时，其中心词决定单复数。

One of my friends is coming to see me.
我的一个朋友准备来看我。
Peter's seemingly effortless flights continue to delight his fans.
彼得看似毫不费力的飞行，继续让他的粉丝们开心。
Mastery of the skills is essential in this job.
在这项工作中，掌握这些技能是很关键的。

4. 一些表示数量的短语

表示复数概念的短语作主语，谓语用复数。

A lot of people are coming here.
许多人将要来这里。
A number of people are coming here.
许多人将要来这里。

表示整体概念的短语作主语，谓语通常用单数，有时也用复数。

A group of students is coming here.
一群学生将要来这里。
A group of students are coming here.
一群学生将要来这里。

表示单数概念的短语作主语，谓语通常用单数。

The number of students is increasing rapidly.
学生的数量正在快速增加。

5. 并列主语

并列主语为一体时，谓语用单数；并列主语为两者或多者时，谓语用复数。

The writer and poet is going to lecture on English learning at our school.
该作家兼诗人准备在我校进行关于英语学习的演讲。
Fish and chips is a traditional dish in England.
炸鱼土豆条在英国是一道传统食物。
You and I are friends.
你和我是好朋友。
What you say and what you do are important.
你说的和你做的都很重要。

当主语是由 as well as 或 together with 等连接的准并列主语时，谓语的单复数应与连接词前的名词保持一致。

The teacher, as well as the students, was eager to know the exam results.
老师，还有学生们，都很急切地想知道考试成绩。
Mary, together with her parents, is going to New York next week.
玛丽，还有她的父母，准备下周去纽约。

6. 就近原则

当主语由 either...or... 或 not only...but also... 等连接时，谓语的单复数应与靠近它的名词保持一致。

Either the students or the teacher is responsible for this.
这些学生们或这位教师要为此负责。
Either the teacher or the students are responsible for this.
这位教师或这些学生们要为此负责。
Not only the teacher but also the students are responsible for this.
不仅这位教师，而且有这些学生都要为此负责。
Not only the students but also the teacher is responsible for this.
不仅这些学生，而且有这位教师都要为此负责。

7. 特殊情况

Three dollars is enough.（3 美元被看作一笔钱）
3 美元足够了。
The audience were enjoying every minute of it.
观众们正津津有味地欣赏着它。
The audience was enormous.
观众非常多。

3.2　时态

时态通常表示动作发生的时间和状态。时态属于谓语动词（包括系动词）的重要功能之一。英语中共有十六个时态（表 3-2）。

表 3-2　英语时态表

时	态			
	一般	进行	完成	完成进行
现在	do/does/am/is/are	am/is/are doing	have/has done	have/has been doing
过去	did/was/were	was/were doing	had done	had been doing
将来	will do/be	will be doing	will have done	will have been doing
过去将来	would do/be	would be doing	would have done	would have been doing

英语中的十六个时态是四个"时"和四个"态"的组合。"时"是指时间范畴，分为现在时、过去时、将来时和过去将来时；四个"态"分别是一般态、进行态、完成时态和完成进行态。

3.2.1　现在时态

现在时态共有四个，分别是一般现在时、现在进行时、现在完成时和现在完成进行时，如表 3-3 所示。

表 3-3　现在时态

时	态			
	一般	进行	完成	完成进行
现在	do/does/am/is/are	am/is/are doing	have/has done	have/has been doing

1. 一般现在时

一般现在时通常表示现在、常态及客观等情况，此时谓语动词根据主语的情况使用原形或第三人称单数形式（be 动词根据主语的情况使用 am、is 或 are）。

It is three o' clock now.

现在是三点。

We often drink tea together.

我们经常一起喝茶。

He is always late.

他总是迟到。

She usually comes to see her mother at the weekend.

她通常周末来看她的妈妈。

The earth goes around the sun.

地球围着太阳转。

Monkeys are mammals.

猴子是哺乳动物。

一般现在时还有一些其他常见用法。

In the book, the writer gives us a vivid description of three characters.（讨论书籍作品时）

在本书中，作者给我们生动描述了三个角色。

If it rains tomorrow, I will not go there with you.（用在条件状语从句中）

如果明天下雨的话，我就不跟你去了。

The man in the picture shows a feeling of satisfaction.（图片说明）

图片里的男人显示出了一种满足感。

The train leaves at ten o' clock tonight.（预定的时间）

火车今晚八点出发。

2. 现在进行时

进行时表示在某个特定的时间正在进行的动作，现在进行时表示此时此刻正在进行的动作，其谓语动词的形式是 be doing（be 动词根据主语的情况使用 am, is 或 are, doing 为动词的现在分词形式）。

I am writing a letter.

我正在写一封信。

Jack is enjoying a talk show.

杰克正在欣赏一个脱口秀。

We are communicating with foreigners in English.

我们正在用英语和外国人交流。

现在进行时还有一些其他常见用法。

I am leaving Beijing tomorrow.（表示将来的情况）

我准备明天离开北京。

You are always complaining.（表达责备的态度）

你总是在抱怨。

3. 现在完成时

现在完成时表示一件过去的事影响到现在、持续到现在，或者兼而有之，其谓语动词的形式是 have done（have 根据主语的情况使用 have 或 has，done 为动词的过去分词形式）。

I have the right to take the toy away because I have paid for it.

我有权利把这个玩具拿走因为我已经付过钱了。（表示影响）

We have been friends for many years.

我们是很多年的朋友了。（表示持续）

I have lived in this house for many years, so I am familiar with every corner of it.

这个房子我住了很多年了，所以每一个角落我都很熟悉。（表示持续和影响）

下面通过一段对话来感受一下现在完成时表示过去的事对现在造成影响的用法。

John: Let's see the movie *Titanic* together.

约翰：我们一起看《泰坦尼克号》这部电影啊。

Jane: No. I have already seen it.（现在完成时）

简：不，我已经看过了。

John: When did you see it?

约翰：你什么时候看的？

Jane: I saw it yesterday.（一般过去时）

简：我昨天看的。

当约翰发出一起看电影的邀请时，简说已经看过了，暗含的意思是不想再看了。很明显，过去的这件事对现在产生了影响。

下面一段对话体现了现在完成时表示过去的事持续到现在的用法。

John: Let's move to Shanghai.

约翰：我们搬家到上海吧。

Jane: Why? I have lived in Beijing for ten years, so I don't agree to move away.

简：为什么？我在北京已经住十年了，所以我不同意搬走。

从上面这个对话中，可以看到简在北京已经住了十年，证明她是从十年前一直住到现在的（动作从过去持续到现在）。

4. 现在完成进行时

现在完成进行时表示一件事从过去一直持续到现在并且仍在进行中，其谓语动词的形式是 have been doing（have 根据主语的情况使用 have 或 has, doing 为动词的现在分词形式）。

I have been doing my homework since 8 a.m..

我从早上八点到现在一直在写家庭作业。

How long have you been playing football?

你踢足球多久了？

We have been practicing the skill for a long time.

我们练习这个技能很长时间了。

We have been studying here since 1999.

我们从 1999 年就开始在这里学习了。

You have been working too hard.

你（一直以来）太努力了。

3.2.2 过去时态

学完现在的四个时态后，再看过去的四个时态（表 3-4）就简单多了。大部分情况下，只需要把时间平移到过去，就可以更容易理解这四个时态的主要用法。

表 3-4　过去时态

时	态			
	一般	进行	完成	完成进行
过去	did/was/were	was/were doing	had done	had been doing

1. 一般过去时

一般过去时用来表示发生在过去的事，谓语动词使用动词的过去式（be 动词根据主语的情况使用 was 或 were），不规则动词的过去式变化方法需要单独记忆。

Jack began to learn English last year.

杰克去年开始学的英语。

He died in 2009.

他于 2009 年去世。

I was there when the accident happened.

事故发生的时候我在那里。

2. 过去进行时

过去进行时表示在过去的某一时刻正在进行的动作，其谓语动词的形式是 was 或 were doing（根据主语的情况使用 was 或 were，doing 为动词的现在分词形式）。

I was having a nap when you called me.

你给我打电话时，我正在睡觉。

I was reading a book at 10 o' clock yesterday morning.

我昨天上午十点正在读一本书。

3. 过去完成时

过去完成时表示先于过去某一时间的动作，或过去某一时间前就已经完成的动作对过去造成的影响，其谓语动词的形式是 had done（done 为动词的过去分词形式）。

Xiaoming had finished the report when his father arrived.

当他的爸爸到达时，小明已经完成了报告。

We had supper together after my father had come back.

我们在我爸爸回来之后一起吃晚饭。

I had lived here for many years, so I knew every corner of the area.

我在这里住了很多年，所以我了解这个地区的每一个角落。

4. 过去完成进行时

过去完成进行时表示从过去的某一时间点持续到过去的另一时间点，并且在这个时间点上还在进行的动作，其谓语动词的形式是 had been doing（doing 为动词的现在分词形式）。

It was 8 o'clock in the evening, and Xiaoming had already been waiting for three hours.

晚上八点了，小明已经等了三小时了。

He had been working on the theory for over twenty years when he published his famous paper.

当他发表他的著名论文时，他已经研究这项理论二十多年了。

3.2.3　将来时态

将来时态共有四个，分别是一般将来时、将来进行时、将来完成时和将来完成进行时，如表 3-5 所示。

表 3-5　将来时态

时	态			
	一般	进行	完成	完成进行
将来	will do	will be doing	will have done	will have been doing

1. 一般将来时

一般将来时最常见的表达方式就是 will do。

I will fly to New York next week.

我下周将要飞往纽约。

You will be punished if you do that.

如果你做那事，你将被惩罚。

Jeromy will be home at 9 o'clock.

杰罗米将会在九点到家。

I shall see you tomorrow.

我明天见你。

助动词 be going to 也是一般将来时的表达方法。它在正式程度上弱于 will do 结构，而且 be going to 往往表示计划、打算，或根据现状判断将要发生的事等。

What are you going to do after the meeting?
你打算会议之后做什么？
It is going to rain soon.
很快要下雨了。

条件状语从句和时间状语从句中有用一般现在时表示将来的情况。

If it rains tomorrow, I will not go there with you.
如果明天下雨，我就不跟你去那儿了。
I will tell him the news when he comes back.
当他回来我会告诉他这个消息。

现在进行时也有表示较近将来的情况。

Jeromy is leaving tomorrow.
杰罗米明天要离开。
We are going to New York soon.
我们很快要去纽约了。

2. 将来进行时
将来进行时通常表示将来某个时刻正在发生的动作，其谓语动词的形式是 will be doing（doing 为动词的现在分词形式）。
下面的对话有助于对将来进行时的理解。

Dad: I will call you at 3 o' clock tomorrow morning.
爸爸：我明天早上三点给你打电话。
Xiaoming: I will be sleeping at 3 o' clock tomorrow morning, so don' t call me then.
小明：我明早三点正在睡觉，所以别在那个时候给我打电话。

从上面这段对话可以看出，小明说明天早上三点（将来的一个时刻）他正在睡觉，所以请他爸爸不要打电话给他。

3. 将来完成时
将来完成时表示截止到将来的某一时间完成的事，其谓语动词的形式是 will have done（done 为动词的过去分词形式）。

By the time you come back, I will have finished the report.
等你回来，我都把报告写完了。

4. 将来完成进行时
将来完成进行时表示一个动作一直持续到将来的某一时间，并且还没有结束，仍在继续，其谓语动词的形式是 will have been doing（doing 为动词的现在分词形式）。

By the time you come back with them, I will have been doing my homework for 8 hours.

等你和他们回来时，我将已经写家庭作业八小时了。

By the end of next month, I will have been teaching in this school for 30 years.

到下个月底，我将在这个学校教学三十年了。

3.2.4　过去将来时态

过去将来时态共有四个，分别是一般过去将来时、过去将来进行时、过去将来完成时和过去将来完成进行时，如表 3-6 所示。过去将来时态的核心就是在过去展望未来的事情。

表 3-6　过去将来时态

时	态			
	一般	进行	完成	完成进行
过去将来	would do	would be doing	would have done	would have been doing

1. 一般过去将来时

一般过去将来时表示从过去的某一时间来看将要发生的动作或呈现的状态，其谓语动词的形式是 would do。

The girl said that she would begin to learn French next year.

这个女孩说他准备明年开始学习法语。

The father told me that he would praise his son.

这位父亲跟我说他准备表扬他的儿子。

2. 过去将来进行时

过去将来进行时是指在过去的某一时间点对进行展望，其谓语动词的形式是 would be doing（doing 为动词的现在分词形式）。

They said that they would be waiting for us on the square when we arrived.

他们说当我们到达的时候，他们将会在广场等着。

I knew that I would be living in China.

我知道我将来会住在中国。

3. 过去将来完成时

过去将来完成时表示在过去的某一时间点展望到将来的某一时间点将要完成的事情，其谓语动词的形式是 would have done（done 为动词的过去分词形式）。

They said that by the time we arrived, they would have finished the report.

他们说当我们到达时，他们将已经完成了报告。

4. 过去将来完成进行时

过去将来完成进行时表示在过去的某一时间点展望到将来的某一时间点做了一段时间但仍在持续的事情，其谓语动词的形式是 would have been doing（doing 为动词的现在分词形式）。

They told me that by the end of next month, they would have been teaching in this school for 30 years.

他们告诉我到下个月底，他们将在这个学校教学三十年了。

Xiaoming said that by the time his father came back, he would have been doing his homework for 8 hours.

小明说等他爸爸回来时，他将已经写家庭作业八小时了。

3.3 被动语态

谓语动词的一个非常重要的功能就是体现被动语态。被动语态的基本结构是 be done (by...)，其中 be 动词属于助动词，done 属于动词的过去分词形式，by 后跟施动方（动作的执行者）。

The apple was eaten by Jack.
那个苹果被杰克吃了。

除了 be 动词外，get 也可以构成被动语态，尤其是在非正式语体中。

You will get punished if you don't stop doing this.
如果你不停止做这件事，你会受到惩罚的。

不及物动词没有被动语态形式，但有些及物动词也没有被动语态形式。

I have many friends.
我有很多朋友。
The essay lacks proper reasoning.
这篇文章缺乏适当的论证。

使用被动语态需要同时注意时态。

How were these houses constructed?
这些房子是如何被建造的？
I am often praised for being willing to help.
我经常因为愿意帮助别人而受表扬。
The bridge is being built.
桥正在被建。

He said that he was being monitored.

他说他正在被监控。

These proposals have been denied.

这些提议已经被否决了。

That candidate suggested that the votes had been miscounted.

那位候选人暗示说选票被统计错了。

3.4 ▶ 否定

虽然句子的很多成分都可以表达否定概念，但谓语动词的否定还是属于主要的否定方式，这是谓语动词的重要功能。

3.4.1 实义动词的否定

实义动词需要加助动词 do 来辅助否定。为了更直观地展示这一点，现将肯定、否定，以及常用的缩写放在一起对比。

I know him.

我认识他。

I do not know him.

I don't know him.

我不认识他。

He belongs to the union.

他属于那个工会。

He does not belong to the union.

He doesn't belong to the union.

他不属于那个工会。

The man spoke to me.

那个男人跟我说话了。

The man did not speak to me.

The man didn't speak to me.

那个男人没跟我说话。

Jane has many friends.

简有很多朋友。

Jane does not have many friends.

Jane doesn't have many friends.
简没有很多朋友。

3.4.2 be 动词的否定

be 动词（包括系动词 be 和助动词 be）否定时在它后面直接加 not。为了直观表现否定的变化，现将肯定、否定，以及常用的缩写放在一起对比。

I am a doctor.
我是医生。
I am not a doctor.
我不是医生。

He is a doctor.
他是医生。
He is not a doctor.
He isn't a doctor.
他不是医生。

They are from France.
他们来自法国。
They are not from France.
They aren't from France.
他们不是来自法国。

That was a good idea.
那是个好主意。
That was not a good idea.
That wasn't a good idea.
那不是个好主意。

They were punished for talking like that.
他们因为那样说话而受罚。
They were not punished for talking like that.
They weren't punished for talking like that.
他们没有因为那样说话而受罚。

在祈使句中，be 动词的否定需要助动词辅助。

Don't be shy.

别害羞。

3.4.3　情态动词的否定

情态动词可以直接在后加 not 进行否定。为了直观表现否定的变化，现将肯定、否定，以及常用的缩写放在一起对比。

The house will be donated to a school.

这栋房子将会被捐赠给一所学校。

The house will not be donated to a school.

The house won't be donated to a school.

这栋房子将不会被捐赠给一所学校。

The boy could speak English when he was little.

这个男孩在很小的时候就会说英语。

The boy could not speak English when he was little.

The boy couldn't speak English when he was little.

这个男孩在很小的时候不会说英语。

有些词被称作"半情态动词"，它们兼有实义动词和情态动词的用法，否定形式不止一种。这类词常见的有 need, dare, used to, ought to 等。

He needs to persuade Jack into buying that car.（实义动词）

他需要劝杰克买那辆车。

He doesn't need to persuade Jack into buying that car.（实义动词）

他不需要劝杰克买那辆车。

He needn't persuade Jack into buying that car.（情态动词）

他不需要劝杰克买那辆车。

知 识 应 用

选择题

1. All we need _____ a small piece of land where we can plant various kinds of fruit trees throughout the growing seasons of the year.

  A. are   B. was   C. is   D. were

2. —Hi, let's go skating.

  —Sorry, I'm busy right now. I _____ in an application form for a new job.

  A. fill   B. have filled   C. am filling   D. will fill

3. My washing machine _____ this week, so I have to wash my clothes by hand.

    A. was repaired   B.is repaired   C.is being repaired   D. has been repaired

4. In the 1950s in the U.S., most families had just one phone at home, and wireless phones _____ yet.

    A. haven' t invented   B. haven' t been invented

    C. hadn' t invented   D. hadn' t been invented

5. Jack _____ in the lab when the power cut occurred.

    A. works   B. has worked   C. was working   D. would work

6. —Can' t you stay a little longer?

    —It' s getting late. I really _____ go now. My daughter is home alone.

    A. may   B. can   C. must   D. dare

7. I love the weekend, because I _____ get up early on Saturdays and Sundays.

    A. needn' t   B. mustn' t   C. wouldn' t   D. shouldn' t

8. —Excuse me, which movie are you waiting for?

    —The new *Star Wars*. We_____ here for more than two hours.

    A. waited   B. wait

    C. would be waiting   D. have been waiting

9. More expressways _____ in Sichuan soon to promote the local economy.

    A. are being built   B. will be built

    C. have been built   D. had been built

10. Since the time humankind started gardening, we _____ to make your environment more beautiful.

    A. try   B. have been trying

    C. are trying   D. will try

四大功能句型

本章继续深入讨论各类句型。句型分类的方法通常包括按照成分分类、功能分类和结构分类等。按照功能分类的四大句型包括陈述句、疑问句、祈使句和感叹句。

4.1 陈述句

陈述句是指通过陈述的方式传递信息的句型。陈述句分为肯定型陈述句和否定型陈述句。还有一个特殊的 There be 句型也在此部分讨论。

4.1.1 肯定型陈述句

肯定型陈述句含义上表示肯定概念。

English is a useful tool.

英语是一个有用的工具。

Michael and his friends often help people in difficulty.

迈克尔和他的朋友们经常帮助有困难的人。

Music can make me relaxed, especially after a hard day's work.

音乐能让我放松，尤其是在一天的辛苦工作之后。

He said that he would come to see me.

他说他会来看我。

It is extremely important to follow the rules.

遵守这些规则极其重要。

4.1.2 否定型陈述句

否定型陈述句含义上表示否定概念，形式上通常是在谓语动词部分进行否定，但还有着其他否定手段，如通过主语或者其他成分进行否定。

Money is not so important.

钱没有那么重要。

I don't know how to play the violin.

我不知道怎么拉小提琴。

John knows nothing about the movie.

约翰对这部电影一无所知。

You mustn't waste your time and energy.

你一定不能浪费时间和精力。

Few people in the company know how to deal with this issue.

该公司里几乎没有人知道如何处理这件事。

4.1.3　There be 存在句型

There be 句型是一种特殊的句型，又被称作"存在句"，通常表示某处存在某物或某人。

There is a cat in the garden.

在花园里有一只猫。

There are three chairs and one desk in the room.

房间里有三把椅子和一张桌子。

There was no one on the plane.

飞机上一个人也没有。

There be 句型的主语通常是 be 动词后面的名词（短语）或代词，所以 be 动词要和其保持一致。

There was something that worried me.

有东西让我担心。

There are some people in the office.

办公室有一些人。

There be 句型中的状语一般分为地点状语、时间状语，以及其他一些表示抽象意义的状语，还有一些不加状语的情况。

Is there a supermarket near here?

这附近有超市吗？

There are twelve months in a year.

一年有十二个月。

There is difficulty in expressing my feelings.

我在表达情感方面有困难。

There is a surprising phenomenon in the society.

社会上有一种令人吃惊的现象。

There has been a misunderstanding between the two sides.

双方存在过分歧。

There is no evidence to support this claim.

没有证据支持这一观点。

There be 句型中的 be 动词还可以由一些其他词替换，包括具有"存在"含义的 live、exist、lie、remain 等；具有"出现"含义的 emerge、arise、occur 等；具有"移动"含义的 come、enter 等。

Long long ago, there lived a king.

很久很久以前，有一个国王。

There exists a quiet small village.

有一个安静的小村庄。

There lie great business opportunities.

有着巨大的商机。

There remains much to be done.

还有很多事要做。

There appeared before them a big mountain.

他们面前出现了一座大山。

There arises a hard question.

出现了一个难题。

With the development of technology, there have emerged new business models.

随着科技的发展，出现了新的商业模式。

There comes a moment when our lives change forever.

那一瞬间使我们的人生永远改变。

There entered three officers.

进来了三位警官。

4.2　疑问句

和陈述句不同，疑问句的主要功能不是提供信息，而是寻求信息。疑问句包括一般疑问句、特殊疑问句、选择疑问句、附加疑问句和修辞疑问句等。本书只讨论常见的类型。

4.2.1　一般疑问句

一般疑问句属于"是否"问句（yes-no question），询问者期望得到肯定或否定的回答。一般疑问句的提问方式是通过将句子的主谓语序倒装来实现的，分为以下三种情况。

1. be 动词

be 动词在疑问时可以直接和主语进行倒装（置于主语前）。一般疑问句的回答采用简略形式（如果回答是否定的，还需要加上 not）。

—Is he a doctor?

他是个医生吗？

—Yes, he is.

是的，他是。

—Are we ready to go?

我们准备好出发了吗？

—No, we are not.

不，我们没有准备好。

—Is there anyone in the classroom?

教室里有人吗？

—Yes, there is.

是的，有人。

—Were you there last night?

你昨晚在那儿吗？

—Yes, I was.

是的，我在。

—Were you chatting with him when I came in?

我进来的时候你在跟他聊天吗？

—No, I wasn't.

不，我没有。

2. 实义动词

除极少数例外，实义动词无法和主语直接进行倒装（无法直接置于主语前），所以需要助动词 do 的辅助。回答也使用简略的形式，即主语加助动词 do 的适当形式即可（如果回答是否定的，还需要加上 not）。

—Do they know how to do it?

他们知道怎么做吗？

—Yes, they do.

是的，他们知道。

—Does John speak English?

约翰说英语吗？

—Yes, he does.

是的，他说（英语）。

—Did you go there last night?

你昨天晚上去那里了吗？

—No, I didn't.

不，我没去。

—Did you finish the report on time?

你们按时完成报告了吗？

—Yes, we did.

是的，我们按时完成了。

3. 情态动词和助动词

情态动词和助动词可以直接和主语进行倒装（情态动词或助动词置于主语前）。

Can you tell me where the nearest bus station is?

你能告诉我最近的公交车站在哪里吗？

Will they consider my advice?

他们会考虑我的建议吗？

Has he gone to the United States?

他去美国了吗？

回答时直接使用主语（注意人称有时需要变化）加相应的情态动词或助动词即可（如果回答是否定的，还需要加上 not）。

—Have you finished your report yet?

你完成你的报告了吗？

—Yes, I have.

是的，我完成了。

—No, I have not.

不，我没完成。

情态动词 must 提问的句子，在肯定和否定回答时有不同。

—Must Jack finish the report today?

杰克必须今天完成这份报告吗？

—Yes, he must.

是的，他必须。

—No, he need not / No, he doesn't have to.

不，他不必。

半情态动词 need 等在作为情态动词使用时移至句首进行提问。

Need you leave so early?

你需要这么早离开吗？

Need I say more about this?

关于这一点，我还需要说更多吗？

4.2.2　特殊疑问句

特殊疑问句借助特殊疑问词对某一具体方面进行提问。特殊疑问词分为疑问代词（如 what, which, who, whom, whose）和疑问副词（如 when, where, why, how）。通常在结构上，特殊疑问词位于句首，后接倒装语序（特殊疑问词作主语时除外）。

What makes you so unique?

是什么让你如此独特？

1. 疑问代词

疑问代词在疑问句中除了表达疑问的具体方面以外，还要承担句子的某个成分。通常来讲，疑问代词承担主语、宾语、表语等功能（其中 what, which 和 whose 可以作代词，也可以作限定词）。

What is Jack doing right now?

杰克现在正在做什么？

What school do you go to?

你上什么学校？

What kind of music do you like?

你喜欢什么样的音乐？

What day is it today?

今天星期几？

Which do you prefer, the big one or the small one?

你更喜欢哪一个，大的那个还是小的那个？

Which books do you like?

你喜欢哪些书？

Which one of you went there last night?

你们当中哪一个人昨天晚上去了那里？

Who helped you when you were in difficulty?

在你困难的时候谁帮了你？

Who(m) did you help last night?

你昨晚帮过谁？

To whom did you tell the story?

你给谁讲了这个故事？

2. 疑问副词

常见的疑问副词有 when, where, why, how（其中 how 既可以单独使用，也可以和一些形容词或副词构成短语一起使用），通常承担状语（或表语）的功能。

When shall we start to learn English?

我们什么时候开始学习英语？

Where did you meet him yesterday?

你昨天在哪里见他的？

Why did you meet him yesterday?

你昨天为什么见他？

How do you feel about this?

对这事你感觉怎么样？

How old are you?

你多大了？

How often do you go to the gym?

你多久去一次健身房？

How long have you been playing football?

你踢球多长时间了？

4.2.3 选择疑问句

选择疑问句在结构上类似一般疑问句，但是内容上不再问"是否"，而是提供两个或多个选项请被提问者选择。

—Are you a teacher or a doctor?

你是教师还是医生？

—I am a teacher.

我是个教师。

选择疑问句还有另一种和特殊疑问句相似的提问方式。

—Which do you prefer, the red one or the blue one?

你更想要哪个？红色的那个，还是蓝色的那个？

—I prefer the blue one.

我更想要蓝色的那个。

4.2.4　附加疑问句

　　附加疑问句是在陈述句后加上一个简单的提问，询问对方是否如此。在提问部分需要使用主谓倒装的结构。通常情况下，前面陈述句用肯定形式，则后面附加疑问句用否定形式；前面陈述句用否定形式，则后面附加疑问句用肯定形式。

　　You are a student, aren't you?

　　你是学生，对吗？

　　You love music, don't you?

　　你喜欢音乐，对吗？

　　Jack can sing many Chinese songs, can't he?

　　杰克能唱很多中文歌，对吗？

　　Jane went there last night, didn't she?

　　简昨天晚上去了那儿，对吗？

　　He hasn't finished his job, has he?

　　他还没有完成工作，对吗？

　　附加疑问句也采用简洁回答。

　　—He loves music, doesn't he?

　　他喜欢音乐，对吗？

　　—Yes, he does.

　　对，他喜欢。

　　—No, he doesn't.

　　不，他不喜欢。

　　在"前否定后肯定"的句式中，Yes 或 No 的选择取决于后面的内容。

　　—You don't love music, do you?

　　你不喜欢音乐，对吗？

　　—No, I don't.

　　对，我不喜欢。

　　—Yes, I do.

　　不，我喜欢。

　　—You didn't go there last night, did you?

　　你昨天没有去那儿，对吗？

　　—No, I didn't.

　　对，我没去。

　　—Yes, I did.

　　不，我去了。

—He hasn't finished his job, has he?

他还没有完成工作，对吗？

—No, he hasn't.

对，他没有。

—Yes, he has.

不，他完成了。

附加疑问句的肯定和否定有时也会出现和前面的陈述句一致的情况，这往往表示问话人对所问的内容比较有把握，倾向性已经比较明显。

You have finished your report, have you?

你已经完成了你的报告，对吗？

祈使句的附加疑问句通常用 will you（语气比较坚决）或 won't you（语气不坚决）来提问。

Open the door, will you?

把门打开，好吗？

4.3　祈使句

祈使句表达请求或者命令。祈使句的典型特征就是不用主语而用谓语动词直接开头（除非特殊情况）。祈使句分为肯定型和否定型。肯定型祈使句用动词原形开头，否定型祈使句通常是在句首直接加 don't 对动词进行否定。

Sit down.

坐下。

Come to my office, please.

请来我的办公室。

Be a man.

像个男人点。

Be quiet.

安静点。

Don't come any closer.

不要再靠近了。

祈使句中的主语有时也可能出现。

—Don't talk anymore. Get out!

别再说了。出去！

—You get out!

你出去!

祈使句也遵守五大句型,也就是根据谓语动词的类型产生以下五种情况(主语被省略)。

(主)+谓
Come.(不及物动词)
过来。
(主)+谓+宾
Help me.(单宾动词)
帮我。
(主)+谓+宾+宾
Tell me a story.(双宾动词)
给我讲个故事。
(主)+谓+宾+宾补
Put it on the table.(宾补动词)
把它放在桌子上。
(主)+系+表
Be quiet.(系动词)
安静。

4.4 感叹句

感叹句通常有两种,即 what 和 how 所引出的句子。在原来陈述句中需要感叹的成分前加上 what 或 how,然后将这部分移到句首,就形成了感叹句。

He is a handsome boy.
他是一个很帅的男孩。
What a handsome boy he is!
他是多么帅的男孩啊!

The boy is handsome.
这个男孩很帅。
How handsome the boy is!
这个男孩多帅啊!

下面来看看每组例子是如何从陈述句变为感叹句的。

You have a nice car.(陈述句)
你有一辆很好的车。

What a nice car you have!（感叹句）
你有一辆多么好的车啊！

Jack runs fast.（陈述句）
杰克跑得很快。
How fast Jack runs!（感叹句）
杰克跑得多快啊！

The house was decorated beautifully.（陈述句）
这栋房子装修得很漂亮。
How beautifully the house was decorated!（感叹句）
这栋房子装修得多漂亮啊！

知识应用

一、选择题

1. —Did you use to have long hair or short hair, Sally?
   —_____.
   A. Yes, I did   B. No, I didn't
   C. Long hair   D. Curly hair

2. —He doesn't speak English or Japanese, _____?
   —_____. He speaks Chinese.
   A. does he; Yes, he doesn't   B. doesn't he; No, he does
   C. does he; No, he doesn't   D. does he; Yes, he does

3. —_____ do you brush your teeth?
   — Twice or more a day.
   A. How soon   B. How far   C. How long   D. How often

4. Please _____ the rubbish into different litter bins according to the signs.
   A. puts   B. put   C. putting   D. to put

5. _____ wake up your sister, Ben. She needs a good sleep.
   A. Don't   B. Doesn't   C. Aren't   D. Can't

6. Guan Dong saved an old lady out of the Yangtze River. _____ great courage he showed!
   A. What a   B. What   C. How a   D. How

7. _____ important it is for kids to imagine freely !
   A. What   B. What a   C. What an   D. How

二、按要求改句子

1. The new product consists of four main parts inside.（改为一般疑问句）

_____

2. Susan followed <u>Ben's</u> advice to design smart shoes.（就画线部分提问）

_____

3. Yao Ming is an excellent Chinese basketball player.（改为感叹句）

_____

三大结构句型

本章从句子结构的角度来讨论三大结构句型，即简单句、并列句和复合句。从结构的角度看，这三种句型涵盖了几乎所有的英语句子。

5.1 简单句

简单句是一种结构上的分类方法，并不代表这类句型特别的简单。事实上，简单句也可能非常复杂，如下面这个例句。

A study by the University of Manchester calculated the emissions of CO_2—the main greenhouse gas responsible for climate change—at every stage of microwaves, from manufacture to waste disposal.（2016 年考研英语二阅读）

简单句只有一套主谓结构，成分的并列不构成并列句，以下结构都属于简单句。因为主语和谓语是句子的决定性因素，所以按照主谓来分类，其他成分可忽略。

1. 主语 + 谓语

I mean it.
我是认真的。
Pumas are fierce animals.
美洲狮是凶猛的动物。
Do you know that boy?
你认识那个男孩吗？

2. 主语 + 主语 + 谓语

Jane and I are getting married.
我和简要结婚了。
Have you and your father been to New York?
你和你父亲去过纽约吗？

Jack and I are not friends.
我和杰克不是朋友。

3. 主语 + 谓语 + 谓语

I waited and waited.
我等啊等。

He jumped to his feet and screamed.
他跳了起来并且大叫。

My sisters sang and danced in my room all day.
我的妹妹们在我的房间里唱啊跳啊一整天。

4. 主语 + 主语 + 谓语 + 谓语

She and I first arrived at the house, and then knocked at the door.
我和她先到了那栋房子，然后敲了门。

The professor and his students invented the tool and sold it to a factory.
教授和他的学生们发明了这个工具，然后卖给了一家工厂。

需要说明的是，成分并列并不限于两个，多个成分也可以并列。

I picked up the phone, talked for a while, and hung up.
我接起电话，聊了一会儿，然后挂了电话。

现在再来看一下前面举过的例子：

A study by the University of Manchester calculated the emissions of CO_2—the main greenhouse gas responsible for climate change—at every stage of microwaves, from manufacture to waste disposal.

这个句子的主干是 "A study calculated the emissions of CO_2."，包含了一个主语 a study 和一个谓语 calculated，所以它也是一个简单句。

5.2 并列句

并列句需要至少两个句子，中间用并列连词连接。并列连词前后两个句子自身都是完整的，而且从结构上看并没有关系（它们之间只存在着逻辑关系）。

The watch was expensive, but I still bought it.
这块表很贵，但我还是买了。

常见的并列连词有七个，它们的首字母可以拼成一个短语 FAN BOYS（for, and, nor, but, or, yet 和 so）。在这七个连词中，and, but 和 or 这三个词最容易归类。它们是最典型的并列连词，既可以连接句子，也可以连接句子成分。

Mary said hello to me, and I smiled to her.

玛丽跟我打了招呼，我对她笑了笑。

I told him to come to the party, but he didn't appear.

我告诉他让他来聚会，但他并没有出现。

Do it now, or we'll be punished.

现在就做，不然我们会受罚的。

连词 for, so, yet 和 nor 在连接句子时更接近并列连词的用法，所以把它们归到此类。

We must learn grammar, for it can help us to understand sentence structures.

我们一定要学语法，因为它能帮我们理解句子结构。

Jack is busy right now, so I am going there myself.

杰克现在很忙，所以我准备自己去。

The house is located in a remote area, yet it is frequently visited.

这栋房子位置偏僻，然而却经常有人光顾。

He didn't go there, nor did I.

他没去那儿，我也没去。

还有一些其他可以连接句子的词或词组。

Jack wants to dance, while Jane wants to sing.

杰克想跳舞，而简想唱歌。

I prefer Spanish as my second foreign language, while he prefers Japanese.

我更倾向于把西班牙语作为我的第二外语，而他却更倾向于日语。

Some people love heavy metal music, whereas others hate it.

有些人喜欢重金属音乐，而有些人却不喜欢。

You think it is not important, whereas I think it is vitally important.

你认为它不重要，我却认为它至关重要。

Not only did John give money to the old man, but he also bought a meal for him.

约翰不仅仅给了这个老人钱，而且给他买了一顿饭。

Either I do it for you, or you do it yourself.

要么我给你做，要么你自己做。

5.3　复合句

复合句是"含有从句的句子"，即用从句而非单词或短语充当复合句的某一成分。主句和从句的关系是包含与被包含的关系，以下几组例句旨在说明该关系。

I know *it*. [1]

I know *that English grammar is important.* [2]

句 [1] 中的 it 是宾语，句 [2] 中的 that English grammar is important 也是宾语，所以它在句 [2] 中的地位，就和 it 在句 [1] 中的地位一样。

It surprised me. [3]
What I saw surprised me. [4]

句 [3] 中的 it 是主语，句 [4] 中的 What I saw 也是主语，所以它在句 [4] 中的地位，就和 it 在句 [3] 中的地位一样。

The *handsome* teacher will come to my home. [5]
The teacher *who is handsome* will come to my home. [6]

句 [5] 中的 handsome 是定语，句 [6] 中的 who is handsome 也是定语，所以它在句 [6] 中的地位，就和 handsome 在句 [5] 中的地位一样。

I saw him *yesterday*. [7]
I saw him *when I was walking in the street*. [8]

句 [7] 中的 yesterday 是状语，句 [8] 中的 when I was walking in the street 也是状语，所以它在句 [8] 中的地位，就和 yesterday 在句 [7] 中的地位一样。

从上面几组例子可以看出，从句就是一个非独立的句子在别的句子里充当一个成分。在后面的部分章节中，我们将按类别讨论从句的构成，以及从句如何在主句里充当成分。

知识应用

请指出下面文章中的各个句子分别是简单句、并列句还是复合句。

Are You Right Handed or Left Handed?

(1) Which hand do you use when you write? (2) About 8 to 15 percent of people are left handed. (3) They often have to use tools that are designed for right-handed people. (4) So it is difficult for left-handers to use most tools. (5) If you are right handed, try this experiment: Take a knife with your left hand and try cutting a potato into pieces. (6) Don't be surprised if you feel awkward.

(7) In the past, people thought it was strange to use the left hand. (8) Young students looked down upon their left-handed classmates. (9) Some children were even punished for using their left hand to write. (10) But these days parents and teachers have accepted that. (11) In almost every school in the world, left-handed students can use their left hand to write.

(12) What causes people to be left handed or right handed? (13) Experts have searched

long and hard on this. (14) They concluded that left-handed people are left handed for the same reason that right-handed people are right handed. (15) One out of every ten people just is a left-hander. (16) It's simply like the color of our eyes—some people have brown eyes, while some others have black eyes.

(17) However, many researchers think that left-handers and right-handers are different in some aspects. (18) Right-handers are more talkative and outgoing than left-handers. (19) Many right-handed people understand spoken words better. (20) For example, after they listen to directions to a supermarket, they can find it easily. (21) Right-handers are good at organizing people, too. (22) They are also better basketball guards. (23) Just ask Yao Ming.

(24) Research shows that left-handers are creative and artistic. (25) Many famous performers, like Jim Carrey and Paul McCartney, are left handed. (26) Many left-handers learn better visually. (27) In art, both Leonardo da Vinci and Michelangelo were left handed. (28) In music, Ludwig van Beethoven was left handed. (29) In science, you find Newton and Einstein. (30) The left-handed people are also really good at tennis and other single sports.

(31) If you prefer one hand, but you are still good at writing with the other, you are mixed handed. (32) Research shows mixed-handers can remember everyday things better than other people. (33) What did you eat for lunch two weeks ago? (34) If you're mixed handed, you can probably remember.

名词性从句

所谓名词性从句，就是其句法功能相当于名词的从句，它在句中承担名词所承担的主要成分包括主语、宾语、表语和同位语等。名词性从句通常分为三类：由 that 引导、由 whether 或 if 引导和由 wh- 词引导。

6.1 由 that 引导

由 that 引导的名词性从句和陈述句关系密切，相当于在陈述句前加上引导词 that 构成。下面几组例子展示了陈述句转化为名词性从句并在其他句子（主句）里充当成分的过程。

English is important.（陈述句）
英语很重要。
that English is important（加 that 变为名词性从句）
We all know *that English is important.*（充当宾语）
我们都知道英语很重要。

Left-handers are creative and artistic.（陈述句）
左撇子有创造力和艺术天赋。
that left-handers are creative and artistic（加 that 变为名词性从句）
Research shows *that left-handers are creative and artistic.*（充当宾语）
研究显示，左撇子有创造力和艺术天赋。

It was strange to use the left hand.（陈述句）
使用左手很奇怪。
that it was strange to use the left hand（加 that 变为名词性从句）
In the past, people thought that it was strange to use the left hand.（充当宾语）
在过去，人们认为使用左手很奇怪。

Mixed-handers can remember everyday things better than other people.（陈述句）

双手灵巧的人比其他人对日常事务记得更牢。

that mixed-handers can remember everyday things better than other people（加 that 变为名词性从句）

Research shows that mixed-handers can remember everyday things better than other people.（充当宾语）

研究显示，双手灵巧的人比其他人对日常事务记得更牢。

由 that 引导的名词性从句在主句中充当的成分通常包括主语、宾语、表语、同位语等。

That Jack loves music is true.（主语从句）

杰克喜欢音乐是真的。

We know *that Jack loves music*.（宾语从句）

我们知道杰克喜欢音乐。

The fact is *that Jack loves music*.（表语从句）

事实是杰克喜欢音乐。

We all know the fact *that Jack loves music*.（同位语从句）

我们都知道杰克喜欢音乐这一事实。

在复合及物动词的宾语后跟形容词作宾语补足语的结构中（谓语 + 宾语 + 宾补），作宾语从句的 that 从句需后置，在原宾语位置用形式宾语 it 替代：

Computers make *it* possible *that people do their jobs with less energy*.

计算机使人们用更少的精力做工作成为可能。

另外，that 引导的名词性从句通常不作介词宾语（除少数例外）。下面的例子使用了 it 作为形式宾语，避免了这个问题。

You should see to *it that everyone is ready at that time*.

你要确保每个人那时都准备好。

关于 that 引导的名词性从句不能作介词宾语，有着一些例外情况，不过这些大都已经被分析为其他类别。例如，在下面这个句子中的 in that 被分析成引导原因状语从句的从属连词。

This book is unusual *in that it offers us special help with our spiritual health*.

这本书很不寻常，因为它给我们提供精神健康方面的特殊帮助。

在正式文体中，在主句表示命令、建议、要求等时，由 that 引导的名词性从句常使用现在时虚拟语气（从句中的谓语动词使用原形）。

It is important *that a scientist know at least a foreign language*.

一名科学家懂至少一门外语是必要的。

We request *that he be freed immediately.*

我们要求他尽快被释放。

He suggested to his mother *that she buy another car.*

他建议他母亲再买一辆车。

The chairman's proposal is *that the project be discussed immediately.*

这位主席的提议是这个项目应该立刻被讨论。

The suggestion *that the meeting be cancelled met with opposition.*

关于取消会议的建议遭到了反对。

6.2 由 whether 或 if 引导

由 whether 或 if 引导的名词性从句保留了一般疑问句或选择疑问句的语义特征。相当于把一般疑问句或选择疑问句通过一些步骤变为名词性从句。下面几组例子展示了这一变化过程。

Is Jack a teacher?（一般疑问句）

杰克是老师吗？

whether/if Jack is a teacher（加 whether 或 if 并将其变为陈述语序使其变为名词性从句）

I don't know *whether Jack is a teacher.*（充当宾语）

我不知道杰克是否是老师。

Did Jack swim in the lake?（一般疑问句）

杰克在湖里游泳了吗？

whether/if Jack swam in the lake（加 whether 或 if 并将其变为陈述语序使其变为名词性从句）

Could you please tell me *whether Jack swam in the lake?*（充当宾语）

能不能请你告诉我杰克是否在湖里游泳了？

Were you there last night?（一般疑问句）

你昨晚在那儿吗？

whether/if you were there last night（加 whether 或 if 并将其变为陈述语序使其变为名词性从句）

I don't know *whether you were there last night.*（充当宾语）

我不知道你昨晚是否在那儿。

Do you use your right hand when you write?（一般疑问句）

你写字时用右手吗？

whether you use your right hand when you write（加 whether 或 if 并将其变为陈述语序使其变为名词性从句）

Tell me *whether you use your right hand when you write*.（充当宾语）

告诉我你写字时是否用右手。

由 whether 引导的名词性从句在主句中充当的成分通常包括主语、宾语、表语、同位语等。

Whether he will help me depends on his schedule.（主语从句）

他是否会帮我取决于他的日程安排。

I don't know *whether he will help me*.（宾语从句）

我不知道他是否会帮我。

That depends on *whether we can carry out our plan*.（介词宾语从句）

那取决于我们是否能实施我们的计划。

My question is *whether he will help me*.（表语从句）

我的问题是他是否会帮我。

The point is *whether they will accept our offer*.（表语从句）

重点是他们是否会接受我们的提议。

There was doubt in the mothers' minds *whether they could find their lost children*.（同位语从句）

妈妈们心中对是否能找到她们丢失的孩子有所怀疑。

和 whether 相比，if 的作用有限，因为 if 还有着引导其他类型从句（如条件状语从句等）的功能，所以有时会有产生歧义的现象。通常，主语从句（后置的主语从句中可以使用 if 引导）、表语从句、介词宾语从句和同位语从句中，不使用 if 引导，而使用 whether 引导。

It is not clear *if he loves music*.

不清楚他是否喜欢音乐。

另外，if 不和 to do 或 or not 连用，这种情况下用 whether；在 or not 后置时，if 和 whether 都可以使用。

I don't know *whether to meet him in person*.

我不知道是否要亲自见他。

I don't know *whether or not I should meet him in person*.

我不知道是否要亲自见他。

I don't know *whether I should meet him in person or not*.

我不知道是否要亲自见他。

I don't know *if I should meet him in person or not*.

我不知道是否要亲自见他。

6.3 由 wh- 词引导

　　由 wh- 词引导的名词性从句和特殊疑问句有着密切的关系。wh- 词和特殊疑问词属于<u>重叠关系</u>，即 what, which, who, whom, whose, when, where, why, how 等。下面几组例子展示了特殊疑问句转化为名词性从句并在其他句子（主句）里充当成分的过程。

Which hand do you use when you write?（特殊疑问句）

你写字时用哪只手？

which hand you use when you write（将其变为陈述语序使其变为名词性从句）

Can you tell me *which hand you use when you write*?（充当宾语）

你能不能告诉我你写字时用哪只手？

What kind of music do you like?（特殊疑问句）

你喜欢什么样的音乐？

what kind of music you like（将其变为陈述语序使其变为名词性从句）

What kind of music you like is not important.（充当主语）

你喜欢什么样的音乐并不重要。

Why did you meet him yesterday?（特殊疑问句）

你为什么昨天见他了？

why you met him yesterday（将其变为陈述语序使其变为名词性从句）

You must explain *why you met him yesterday*.（充当宾语）

你必须解释为什么昨天见他了。

How long have you been playing football?（特殊疑问句）

你踢了多长时间的球？

how long you have been playing football（将其变为陈述语序使其变为名词性从句）

That depends on *how long you have been playing football*.（充当宾语）

那取决于你踢了多长时间的球。

如果特殊疑问句本身没有倒装，则不需要再调整语序。

Who helped you when you were in difficulty?（特殊疑问句）

谁在你困难的时候帮助了你？

who helped you when you were in difficulty（直接变为名词性从句）

We want to know *who helped you when you were in difficulty*.（充当宾语）

我们想知道谁在你困难的时候帮助了你。

　　由 wh- 词引导的名词性从句在主句中充当的成分通常包括主语、宾语、表语、同位语、介词宾语、宾语补足语等。

When we shall start to learn English has not been decided yet.（主语从句）
我们应该什么时候开始学英语还没有决定。

Tell me *how old you are*.（宾语从句）
告诉我你多大了。

My question is *where you met him yesterday*.（表语从句）
我的问题是你昨天在哪里遇见他的。

Please answer the question *why you met him yesterday*.（同位语从句）
请回答你昨天为什么见他这个问题。

That depends on *how much money you have*.（介词宾语从句）
那取决于你有多少钱。

You can call me *whatever you like*.（宾语补足语从句）
你想叫我什么都可以。

还有一类名词性从句并不表示疑问，如在 "What we did last night was not important." 中，what 相当于在 "The thing that we did last night was not important." 中的 the thing that，或者相当于在 "That which we did last night was not important." 这个句子中的 that which。下面列举的例句就属于这种情况。

I drank what was left in the cup.
我喝了杯子里剩余的东西。

We eat what we can; what we can't, we can.
我们吃我们能吃的；我们不能吃的，我们把它装罐子里。

This is where he lives.
这是他住的地方。

What we don't have seems more valuable than what we have.
我们没有的东西似乎比我们拥有的东西更珍贵。

I will choose who(m) I like.
我要选我喜欢的人。

I will choose which I like.
我要选我喜欢的东西。

This is how the world works.
这就是世界运行的方式。

名词性从句的 wh- 引导词有几个可以加上 -ever，表示"任何……"，也可以表示"无论……"。从语法功能上讲，这类引导词引导的从句既可以充当名词性从句，也可以充当让步状语从句。本章主要讲述这类词引导的名词性从句。

I believe *whatever you say*.

我相信你说的所有的话。

Please do *whatever is required and do it well.*

请按照要求去做，并且把它做好。

Whoever breaks the law will be punished.

任何犯法的人都会受到惩罚。

The government will provide assistance for *whoever takes this job.*

政府会给任何接受这项工作的人提供帮助。

We all have the right to love *whomever we choose.*

我们都有权利去爱我们选择的人。

Whichever of you finishes the report first will get rewarded.

你们当中谁先完成报告谁就会得到奖赏。

6.4 直接引语和间接引语

除了表达自己的所思所想外，人们有时需要转述别人的所思所想。转述的方法可能是直接不加改变地使用别人的原话，这就是直接引语；也可能是加工一下变成自己的口吻，这就是间接引语。

6.4.1 直接引语

直接引语是指说话人直接引述别人的原话，放在引号里不加任何改变。直接引语常放在包括 say, ask, answer, tell, beg, argue, reply, announce, comment, shout, state, warn, whisper, promise, cry, insist, confess 等词之后。

直接引语中的转述句式有三种位置，可以放在句首、句尾和句中。

1. 位于句首

He said, "I will help you."

他说："我会帮你的。"

Jack replied, "I am so happy to see you."

杰克回答道："很开心见到你。"

He commented, "It is an excellent movie."

他评价道："这是一部优秀的电影。"

The policeman warned us, "Don't go out at night."

那个警察警告我们说："不要晚上出去。"

The teacher asked, "What are you going to do?"

这位老师问道："你们打算做什么？"

The boys shouted, "What a nice boat it is!"

这些男孩喊道："这是多么棒的船啊！"

2. 位于句尾

"My mother will come here to see me," Jack said.

"我母亲会来这里看我，"杰克说道。

"The boss is coming," he whispered.

"老板要来了，"他低声道。

当句子是一般过去时和一般现在时时，主谓通常可以倒装（主语是代词时不倒装）。

"My mother will come here to see me," says Jack.

"我母亲会来这里看我，"杰克说。

"Shall we go now?" asked Mr. Smith.

"我们现在走吧？"史密斯先生问道。

3. 位于句中

"I don't know," Johnson said, "whether I should buy the book."

"我不知道，"约翰说，"我是否该买这本书。"

"I don't know," said Johnson, "whether I should buy the book."

"我不知道，"约翰说，"我是否该买这本书。"

6.4.2　间接引语

除了直接引述别人的原话外，还可以转述，此时需要把句式（如陈述句、疑问句等）或一些成分（如主语的人称、谓语的时态、状语的方位等）转换为合适的形式。

如果直接引语是陈述句，那么把它变为间接引语就相当于把它变为宾语从句。

He said, "I will help you."

他说："我会帮你的。"

He said that he would help me.

他说他会帮我的。

He commented, "It is an excellent movie."

他评价道："这是一部优秀的电影。"

He commented that it was an excellent movie.

他评价说这是一部优秀的电影。

如果直接引语是一般疑问句，也是将一般疑问句变为宾语从句（名词性从句）。

A girl asked, "Can you help me?"

一个女孩问道："你能帮我吗？"

A girl asked whether I could help her.

一个女孩问我是否能帮她。

"Did you swim alone in the lake?" asked my mother.

"你是不是一个人在湖里游泳了？"我母亲问道。

My mother asked (me) whether I swam alone in the lake.

我母亲问（我）我是不是一个人在湖里游泳了。

选择疑问句和一般疑问句的句式相同，转变方式也相同。

"Will you stand beside us or not?" asked the committee members.

"你支持不支持我们？"委员会成员们问道。

The committee members asked (me) whether I would stand beside them or not.

委员会成员们问我支持不支持他们。

把直接引语中的特殊疑问句变成间接引语和名词性从句的变化方法是一样的，即疑问倒装语序变为陈述语序。

"Why is it so unfair to me?" she wondered.

"为什么对我这么不公平？"她想知道。

She wondered why it was so unfair to her.

她想知道为什么对她这么不公平。

祈使句中由于主语被省略了，所以在把直接引语变为间接引语时，有两种句式可以使用，一个是把祈使句变为 to do 不定式；一个是补充主语，使它成为陈述语序。

"Finish the report on time," my boss said to me.

"按时完成这份报告，"我的老板跟我说道。

My boss told me to finish the report on time.

我的老板让我按时完成这份报告。

My boss said that I should finish the report on time.

我的老板说我要按时完成这份报告。

感叹句本身没有倒装（只有被感叹的部分置于句首），所以句式方面无须变化。

The boys shouted, "What a nice boat it is!"

这些男孩喊道："这是多么棒的船啊！"

The boys shouted what a nice boat it was.

这些男孩喊道这是多么棒的船。

"How fast the car runs!" the boy exclaimed.

"这辆车跑得真快！"这个男孩惊呼道。

The boy exclaimed how fast the car ran.

这个男孩惊呼这辆车跑得真快。

除了句式的变化外，在把直接引语变为间接引语时还要考虑很多其他方面的变化，如人称代词、时态、时间状语、地点状语等。接下来通过一个实例来展示需要注意的变化。

Oh, my! Today is May 24th. On May 1st, my father telephoned me and said, "*Come* to *my* office *tomorrow*." I forgot it completely. What to do now? My father told me to *go* to *his* office *the next day*. But I didn't. Oh my!

可以看出，这段话里的间接引语产生了三处变化：动词根据方位进行了变化（come 变为 go）、物主代词进行了变化（my 变为 his）和时间状语进行了变化（tomorrow变为 the next day）。下面一些例子分别展示了人称、时态、时间状语、地点状语和指示代词的变化。

直接引语变为间接引语后，要根据转述人和被转述人的关系进行人称的转换。

He said, "I will start to learn English."
他说："我要开始学英语。"
He said that he would start to learn English.
他说他要开始学英语。

"Will you help me?" asked Joan.
"你能帮我吗？"琼问道。
Joan asked whether I would help her.
琼问我是不是能帮她。

直接引语变为间接引语后，要根据转述句里（主句）的时态进行调整。

Jack replied, "I am so happy to see you."
杰克回答道："很开心见到你。"
Jack replied that he was so happy to see me.
杰克回答说他很开心见到我。

时态也有不变的情况，如转述的内容是客观真理、自然规律等。

Our teacher said to us, "Metal expands when heated."
我们的老师告诉我们说，"金属遇热膨胀。"
Our teacher told us that metal expands when heated.
我们的老师告诉我们金属遇热膨胀。

The tour guide explained, "The sun always shines in this area throughout the year."
这个导游解释道："这个地区太阳终年照耀。"

The tour guide explained that the sun always shines in this area throughout the year.
这个导游解释道这个地区太阳终年照耀。

根据说话人和转述人方位的不同，地点状语和指示代词需要相应的变化。如果转述人和说话人不在一个地方，动词和指示代词可能因此而改变。

He said to me, "Come here to visit this museum."
他跟我说道："来这里参观这个博物馆。"
He told me to go there to visit that museum.
他让我去那里参观那个博物馆。

知识应用

选择题

1. I truly believe _____ beauty comes from within.
    A. that   B. where   C. what   D. why

2. This is _____ my father has taught me — to always face difficulties and hope for the best.
    A. how   B. which   C. that   D. what

3. Every year, _____ makes the most beautiful kite will win a prize in the Kite Festival.
    A. whatever   B. whoever
    C. whomever   D. whichever

4. The manager put forward a suggestion _____ we should have an assistant. There is too much work to do.
    A. whether   B. that
    C. which   D. what

5. _____ Li Bai, a great Chinese poet, was born is known to the public, but some won't accept it.
    A. That   B. Why   C. Where   D. How

6. She asked me _____ I had returned the books to the library, and I admitted that I hadn't.
    A. when   B . where   C. whether   D . what

7. _____ we understand things has a lot to do with what we feel.
    A. Where   B . How   C. Why   D . When

8. Mr. Jackson hasn't decided _____ this weekend.
    A. where he will have a picnic   B. where will he have a picnic
    C. where he had a picnic   D. where did he have a picnic

9. We're discussing why _____ for our health.

    A. are fast food bad   B. fast food are bad

    C. fast food is bad   D. is fast food bad

10. —I'd like to know _____ for the party.

    —I have no idea.

    A. why did she buy so little food   B. what she has prepared

    C. whether will she dance   D. when is she leaving

定 语 从 句

定语从句又被称为形容词性从句。和名词性从句可以承担多种成分不同，形容词性从句在句子里只作定语，所以常被直接称为定语从句。本章根据实际需要混合使用形容词性从句和定语从句这两种名称。

7.1　定语从句的作用

和形容词作定语相似，定语从句的主要作用是修饰或限定先行词（名词或代词等）。使用从句作定语的主要原因之一是可以使表达的内容更加丰富。下面的例子分别是形容词作定语、介词短语作定语和形容词性从句作定语。

I know a *handsome* boy.（形容词作定语）
我认识一个很帅的男孩。
I ate the apple *on the table*.（介词短语作定语）
我吃了桌子上的苹果。
I like the boy *who helped me*.（形容词性从句作定语）
我喜欢那个帮助过我的男孩。
I miss the village *in which I was born*.（形容词性从句作定语）
我怀念那个我出生的村庄。

7.2　定语从句的构成

从本质上讲，定语从句是用一个句子来修饰或限定先行词。但它和形容词等直接作定语有两点不同：①修饰先行词的句子有一个条件，即句子中含有该先行词（或其相应的代词或副词等）。②这个句子需要变化成为从句后才可以修饰或限定先行词。

以名词 the boy 和句子"The boy helped me."为例，该句中含有被修饰名词 the boy，于是就有了修饰它的可能。具体方法是把句中的 the boy 换成相应的关系词即可使该句子成为从句修饰或限定名词：the boy *who helped me*.

如果关系词并非主语，还需要将它移至句首。以名词 the boy 和 "I helped him." 为例，此时的 him 需要变换为关系词后再置于句首：the boy *whom I helped.* 以下各组例句展示了这一变化过程。

the gift（名词）
You gave me *the gift.*（句子）
the gift *which you gave me*（变换为从句修饰名词）

the book（名词）
I bought *it.*（句子）
the book *that I bought*（变换为从句修饰名词）

the woman（名词）
I met *her.*（句子）
the woman *whom I met*（变换为从句修饰名词）

注意名词在句子中的具体成分才能根据它的成分进行和关系词的替换。
the car（名词）
Its doors were broken.（句子）
the car *whose doors were broken*（变换为从句修饰名词）

the village（名词）
I was born *there.*（句子）
the village *where I was born.*（变换为从句修饰名词）

当句中的名词属于短语的一部分时，则该短语在名词替换后整体移至从句首，尤其在正式语体中。

the city（名词）
I live in *the city.*（句子）
the city *in which I live*（变换为从句修饰名词）

the girl（名词）
I bought a dress for *her.*（句子）
the girl *for whom I bought a dress*（变换为从句修饰名词）

the house（名词）
The windows of *it* are broken.（句子）
the house *the windows of which are broken*（变换为从句修饰名词）

在非正式语体中，和关系词构成短语的介词通常可以保留在后，但仍有些介词不可放后。

the person
I spoke to him.
the person who(m) I spoke *to*（介词保留在后）

a long period
We could not talk during the period.
a long period *during* which we could not talk（介词移前）

7.3 ▸ 定语从句的引导词

定语从句的引导词分为关系代词 that, which, who, whom, whose 和 as 等，以及关系副词 when, where, 和 why 等。其中，关系代词通常在从句中作主语、宾语或表语等成分，关系副词通常在从句中作状语等成分。

表示人称的 who 和 whom 通常指人。在限定性定语从句中，who（主格）通常可以替换 whom（宾格），但在介词后时仍需要用宾格形式。

I don't know the person *who spoke to me.*
我不认识那个跟我说话的人。
I don't know the person *who (m) I spoke to.*
我不认识那个我跟他说话的人。
I don't know the person *to whom I spoke.*
我不认识那个跟我说话的人。

表示物称的 which 通常指物，或句子（引导非限定定语从句时）。

The books *which inspired me with courage* are now nowhere to be found.
那些给了我勇气的书现在都找不到了。
The gift *which my mother gave me* was nice.
我母亲给我的礼物很好。
I want to visit Beijing, *which is the capital of China.*
我想参观北京，它是中国的首都。
Mary came home late, *which upset her parents.*
玛丽回家很晚，这让她的父母很苦恼。

表示中性的 that（通常不引导非限定性定语从句且不与介词连用）和 whose 既可以指人，也可以指物。

Many elements *that make up the foundation of the modern world* originated in China.

构成现代世界基础的许多元素都起源于中国。

I know the woman *that won the contest.*

我认识那个赢得了比赛的女士。

先行词既包含人又包含物时，引导词通常用 that。

She misses the people and the things *that gave her so much pleasure.*

她想念那些给了她如此多乐趣的人和事。

当先行词是不定代词 something, everything, nothing, all, much, little 等时，引导词通常用 that。

There is nothing *that we can do.*

没什么我们能做的。

All *that you change* changes you.

你所改变的一切也改变你。

The book contains much *that we don't know.*

这本书里包含很多我们不知道的东西。

There is little *that I can do.*

我做不了什么。

当先行词被最高级形容词或 only 修饰，或被 first, last, next 等修饰时，引导词通常用 that。

She is the most intelligent woman *that I have ever met.*

她是我见过的最聪明的女士。

He is the first astronaut *that travelled in space.*

他是第一个遨游过太空的宇航员。

The last thing *that I want to do* is hurt you.

伤害你是我最不愿意做的事。

whose 是属格形式，既可以指人，也可以指物。

The man *whose drawing we are admiring* is Jack.

那个我们正在欣赏他画作的人是杰克。

He sold the car *whose doors were broken.*

他把那辆门坏了的车卖了。

表中性的 as 既可以指人，也可以指物，还可以在引导非限定性定语从句时指句子。

He is not the same man *as he used to be.*

他不再是从前的那个他了。

It was such a sight *as he had never seen.*

这是他从未见过的景象。

He is the best singer in the group, *as it seems.*

似乎他是团体中最好的歌手。

As we all know, sport brings smile to everyone.

众所周知，体育会带给大家欢乐。

As is demonstrated in the picture, the situation is getting worse.

如图所示，情况正变得更加糟糕。

关系副词主要包括 when（时间），where（地点），why（原因）等。

There are times *when I miss my family.*

有时候我想念我的家人。

The village *where I was born* is beautiful.

那个我出生的村庄很美。

That was the reason *why I took the examination.*

那就是我参加那个考试的原因。

除了关系副词外，"介词 + 关系代词"的结构也可以实现同样的目的。

Mary is the girl *for whom I bought the dress.*

玛丽是我给她买裙子的那个女孩。

The boss fired the sales manager, *for which mistake he paid a price.*

这位老板把销售经理开除了，为此错误他付出了代价。

Pens are tools *with which we write.*

钢笔是我们用来写字的工具。

Do you know the boy *with whom I went to the park?*

你认识那个跟我一起去公园的男孩吗？

A scientist invented the telescope, *with which he studied the sky.*

一位科学家发明了这台望远镜，他用此来研究天空。

There was a long period *during which we could not talk.*

有很长一段时间我们不能谈话。

The Han Dynasty, *during which lots of achievements and accomplishments were made*, is one of the most important dynasties in Chinese history.

汉朝是中国历史上最重要的朝代之一，在此期间有很多显著的成就。

We finally arrived at the farmhouse, *in front of which sat a small boy.*

我们最终到达了那所农舍，农舍前面坐了一个小男孩。

We saw two high buildings, *in the midst of which lay a small house.*

我们看到了两栋高楼，之间还坐落着一所小房子。

The tundra fires in 2012 produced great amounts of soot, *some of which drifted over Greenland and then fell as particles onto the ice sheet.*

2012 年的大火产生了大量的烟尘，有些烟尘飘到了格陵兰岛上空，然后形成微粒，落在了冰盖上。

在修饰表示方式或时间的先行词时，that 也可以作为关系副词引导定语从句，其作用相当于相应的"关系副词或介词 + 关系代词"结构。下面两组例子可以用于对比。

I remember the day *(that)* he left.
我记得他离开的那一天。
I remember the day *when* he left.
我记得他离开的那一天。
I remember the day *on which* he left.
我记得他离开的那一天。

I don't like the way *(that)* she talks.
我不喜欢她谈话的方式。
I don't like the way *in which* she talks.
我不喜欢她谈话的方式。

7.4　限定性定语从句和非限定性定语从句

定语从句分为限定性定语从句和非限定性定语从句。限定性定语从句的作用是在某类事物中确定要谈论的对象。

I like eating bananas *which are grown in Hainan.*
我喜欢吃在海南种植的香蕉。

香蕉是一个大的范围，而 which are grown in Hainan 就把对象限定为"在海南种植"的香蕉。

The book *which I bought* was interesting.
那本我买的书很有意思。

同样，书也是很大的范围，定语从句 which I bought 起到了限定谈论对象的作用。
而非限定性定语从句的作用是补充更多的信息。如果先行词自身已经很明确，或者并未在某类事物中确定要谈论的对象，则使用非限定性定语从句。

I want to visit Beijing, *which is the capital of China.*
我想参观北京，它是中国的首都。
Mary's mother, *who is a doctor,* will come to see her this weekend.

玛丽的妈妈是个医生，这个周末会来看她。

The woman missed her father, *from whom she had no news for a long time.*

这位女士想念她的父亲，她很久都没有他的消息了。

上面的例子中，北京、母亲和父亲自身都很明确，无须限定，所以使用非限定性定语从句。

下面几组例子有助于区分限定性定语从句和非限定性定语从句。

The apples *that were on the table* were picked by Jack.

桌子上的那些苹果是杰克摘的。

The apples, *which were on the table*, were picked by Jack.

那些苹果是杰克摘的，它们在桌子上。

The girls *who were willing to help* came the next morning.

愿意帮忙的女孩子们第二天一早来了。

The girls, *who were willing to help*, came the next morning.

女孩子们愿意帮忙，她们第二天一早来了。

There are twenty children in my class. The children *who wanted to play soccer* went to the park yesterday.

我们班有二十个孩子。昨天，想踢足球的孩子们去了公园。

There are twenty children in my class. The children, *who wanted to play soccer*, went to the park yesterday.

我们班有二十个孩子。昨天，孩子们想踢足球，所以去了公园。

非限定性定语从句还可以修饰句子。

She came home late last night, *which upset her parents.*

她昨晚回家晚，这让她的父母很生气。

He appeared at the meeting, *as was expected.*

正如预料的那样，他出现在了会议上。

As we all know, English grammar is important.

众所周知，英语语法很重要。

知 识 应 用

选择题

1. Jack likes being with the classmates _____ are outgoing and kind.
      A. where   B. which   C. when   D. who

2. I like the city _____ the people are really kind and friendly.

    A. that   B. which   C. where   D. who

3. I hate the dogs _____ live in the next house. They make loud noises all night.

    A. who   B. that   C. what   D. whom

4. Theaters may have a brighter future if they can provide a movie experience _____ people cannot get at home.

    A. that   B. who   C. whom   D. what

5. Being blind is something _____ most people can't imagine.

    A. /   B. what   C. who   D. which

6. Kate, _____ sister I shared a room with when we were at college, has gone to work in Australia.

    A. whom   B. that   C. whose   D. her

7. We will put off the picnic in the park until next week, _____ the weather may be better.

    A. that   B. where   C. which   D. when

8. Scientist have advanced many theories about why human beings cry tears, none of _____ has been proved.

    A. whom   B. which   C. what   D. that

9. The books on the desk, _____ covers are shiny, are prizes for us.

    A. which   B. what   C. whose   D. that

10. English is a language shared by several diverse cultures, _____ uses it differently.

    A. all of which   B. each of which

    C. all of them   D. each of them

第8章

状 语 从 句

状语从句属于副词性从句。状语从句通常包括时间状语从句、地点状语从句、条件状语从句、目的状语从句、原因状语从句、结果状语从句、方式状语从句、比较状语从句和让步状语从句等。从属连词是状语从句的重要构成手段。

8.1 时间状语从句

时间状语从句的常用引导词包括 when, whenever, while, as, as soon as, once, before, after, since, until, till, immediately, directly, no sooner... than..., hardly... when..., scarcely... when..., the minute, the moment, next time, by the time, every time 等。

When I was walking in the street, I met Tom.
当我在街上散步的时候，遇到了汤姆。
Whenever Jack sees his maths teacher, he feels nervous.
杰克每次看到他的数学老师，他都很紧张。
Remember to lock the door whenever you leave the house.
任何时候离开这个房子，记得把门锁上。
We become mature as we grow old.
随着我们变老，我们也变得成熟。
As the moon rises, the air gets cool.
随着月亮升起，空气变得凉爽。
I will tell him the news as soon as he comes back.
他一回来我就告诉他这个消息。
I had already known her before you met her.
在你见她之前我就认识她了。
He went to Beijing after he graduated from the University of Virginia.
他从弗吉尼亚大学毕业后去了北京。
We haven't met Jane since she left last year.

自从简去年离开，我们再也没有见过她。

We will stay in Hong Kong until you find your lost wallet.

我们会一直待在香港，直到你找到丢失的钱包。

I will wait here till he comes back.

我要在这里等到他回来。

She didn't go home until her colleagues came back to the office.

她一直到同事们回到办公室才回家。

Inform me immediately you finish the job.

做完工作后立刻通知我。

He burst into tears directly he heard the news.

他听到消息后立刻大哭起来。

I will tell her the news the minute she comes back.

她一回来我就告诉她这个消息。

I want to talk to her about this the moment she arrives.

我想她一到就跟她讨论这件事。

Next time you go shopping, remember to buy some milk powder.

下一次你去购物时，记得买点奶粉。

By the time we arrived, he had already finished the job.

等我们到的时候，他已经完成了工作。

Every time I see you, you are eating something.

每次我看到你，你都在吃东西。

I had no sooner left the house than it began to rain.

我刚出屋子就开始下雨了。

I had scarcely left the house when it began to rain.

我刚出屋子就开始下雨了。

当 no sooner, hardly 或 scarcely 置于句首时，会引起主句的倒装。

No sooner had I left the house than it began to rain.

我刚出屋子就开始下雨了。

Scarcely had I left the house when it began to rain.

我刚出屋子就开始下雨了。

8.2　地点状语从句

地点状语从句一般表示位置或方向，主要由 where 和 wherever 引导。

You can go where you please.

你可以去你想去的地方。

Where there is smoke, there is fire.

有烟的地方就有火（事出有因）。

We can meet where we first met.

我们可以在我们第一次遇见的地方见面。

wherever 在引导地点状语从句时，常常兼有让步的含义。

You can sit wherever you like.

你喜欢坐哪里就坐哪里。

Wherever he goes, he makes friends.

他去哪里都交朋友。

8.3 条件状语从句

条件状语从句是指主句中的情况是以从句中的情况为条件的，即满足了从句中的情况，主句中的情况才会实现或发生。条件状语从句的常用引导词包括 if, unless, once, so long as, as long as, in case, supposing that, assuming that, on assumption that, given that, provided that, providing that, granted that, granting that, on condition that 等。

If you work hard, you will find that English is not difficult.

你如果努力，你就会发现英语不难。

I will go there with you if it doesn't rain tomorrow.

如果明天不下雨的话，我就跟你一起去那里。

You will find that English is difficult unless you work hard.

你会发现英语很难，除非你努力。

He won't do that unless you tell him to.

除非你告诉他，否则他不会做的。

Once you talk to him in person, you will feel his sincerity.

一旦你亲自和他谈话，你就会感觉到他的真诚。

Once the night comes on, the nocturnal birds in this area will come out.

一旦夜幕降临，这个地区的夜行鸟类就会出来。

In case he comes here, give this wallet to him.

万一他来这里，把这个钱包给他。

Let me know in case you need help.

如果你需要帮助，就告诉我。

So long as trees can grow in the area, man can survive.

只要植物在这个地区能生长，人就能生存。

As long as he lives, he will not forget this experience.

只要他活着，他就不会忘记这次经历。

You can borrow my car on condition that you return it this afternoon.

只要你下午能还给我，你就可以借我的车。

I will hold a party in my yard tomorrow provided/providing that the weather is fine.

如果天气好，我明天将在我的院子里举办一场聚会。

Given that she likes babies, she will be a good mother.

考虑到她喜欢小孩，她会成为一个好母亲。

Assuming that she likes babies, then she should have one of her own.

假设她喜欢小孩，她应该自己生一个。

Supposing that he is in the office now, shall we go there directly to meet him?

假设他现在在办公室，我们该直接去见他吗？

当讲话人认为从句中的条件不可能实现或发生，则使用过去时虚拟语气，即使用过去的形式表示现在和将来，用过去完成的形式表示过去。其中，使用 were 表示 be 动词的虚拟语气。

对现在情况的假设。讲话人认为现在的事实并不符合假设的条件，所以主句中的情况也不会发生。

If I were you, I would not do that.

如果我是你，我就不会做那件事。

If I were in your shoes, I would talk to him immediately.

如果我处在你的位置，我会立刻和他谈。

If our maths teacher were here, we could consult her about the question.

如果我们数学老师在，我们就能请教她这个问题了。

对过去情况的假设。讲话人认为假设的条件在过去并没有发生，所以主句中的情况也就没有发生。

If he had listened to me, he would have succeeded.

如果他听了我的，他本会成功的。

If you had come earlier, I could have told you about it.

如果你早点来，我就能告诉你这事了。

It would have been better if he had shouted to the boy.

他要是大声向这个男孩喊就更好了。

对将来情况的假设。讲话人认为假设的条件在将来并不会发生，所以主句中的情况也不会发生。

If the desert were to disappear tomorrow, there would be no dust storm in our city.

如果明天这片沙漠消失，我们的城市就不会有沙尘暴了。

If he were to win this election, his measures might push the economy down further.

如果他赢得此次选举，他的措施可能会将经济继续推向恶化。

If you came tomorrow, you would receive a warm welcome.
如果你明天来，你会受到热情欢迎。

有时也会出现混合时间的情况，此时从句和主句分别使用相应的形式。

If you had worked hard at that time, you would be a very successful man now.
如果那时你特别努力，现在会是一个很成功的人。

If he had set out earlier, he would be here now.
如果他出发早点，他现在就会在这里了。

If you had listened to the doctor, you would be all right now.
如果你当初听了医生的话，现在就该好了。

谓语部分可能出现倒装现象（had, were 或 should 倒装），并且把引导词省略掉。

Had I known, I would have helped you.
如果我知道，我会帮助你的。

Were it not for your help, I would not have succeeded.
如果不是你的帮助，我不会成功的。

Should you change your mind, I would understand you.
如果你改变主意，我会理解你的。

8.4 目的状语从句

目的状语从句的常用引导词包括 in order that, so that, for fear that, lest 等。

Her parents moved to New York in order that they could take care of her.
她的父母搬到了纽约以便能够照顾她。

We helped him so that he could win the competition.
我们帮助他以便他能赢得比赛。

Jane threw away the knives for fear that her children might get hurt.
简扔掉了这些小刀，以免她的孩子们受伤。

We dare not climb onto the wall lest we should get hurt.
我们不敢爬上墙，恐怕受伤。

在一些目的状语从句中也可能出现虚拟语气，如从属连词 lest, in case 等引导的目的状语从句，从句的谓语动词使用 should 加动词原形，或者直接使用动词原形。

I explained my idea to them lest there (should) be any misunderstanding.
我向他们解释了我的想法以免有误解。

They equipped themselves with the latest weapons lest they (should) be attacked on the road.

他们装备了最新的武器以防路上被攻击。

She keeps her voice low lest she (should) disturb her parents.

她压低声音以免打扰到她的父母。

in case 引导的目的状语从句，在表示可能性比较低的情况下，可以使用 should 加动词原形的谓语形式；在表示可能性高的情况下，可以使用陈述语气。

Learn more skills about your career in case you should lose your current job.

多学习一些和职业相关的技能，以免丢了现在的工作。

Take an umbrella in case it rains.

带一把雨伞，以防下雨。

8.5 ▶ 原因状语从句

原因状语从句的常用引导词包括 because, since, as, in that, now that, seeing that 等。

I didn't go out because it rained.

因为下雨了，我昨晚没有出去。

I bought the book because it attracted me.

我买了这本书因为它吸引了我。

Since it is raining outside, I don't want to go out.

既然外面正在下雨，我就不想出去了。

As it is Sunday, the shops are all closed.

由于是星期天，所以商店都关门了。

He is special to me in that he knows a lot about the history of my hometown.

他对我很特殊，因为他知道很多关于我家乡的历史。

Now that you have already known the story, it is not necessary to relate it.

既然你已经知道这个故事了，就没必要讲了。

Seeing that Jack is so busy with the report, we will not give him additional work.

既然杰克忙着这份报告，我们就不给他增加更多的工作了。

由 because 引导的从句也可以充当表语。

Maybe it is because they lack experience.

也许是因为他们缺乏经验。

8.6 ▶ 结果状语从句

结果状语从句的常用引导词包括 so... that, such... that 等。

I got up so early that I caught the first train.
我起床如此之早以至于我赶上了首班车。

He spoke English so fast that I couldn't understand him.
他英语说得如此之快以至于我无法理解他。

The building is 200 meters tall so that I have to use the elevator.
这栋楼高达 200 米，所以我不得不坐电梯。

Tom is such a handsome boy that girls in the group all like him.
汤姆如此之帅以至于组内的女孩们都喜欢他。

8.7 方式状语从句

方式状语从句的引导词包括 as, as if, as though 等。

You should do it as I have told you.
你应该按照我告诉你的方式做。

He talks as if he is angry.
他谈话时好像生气了似的。

just as..., so... 这个结构比较具有文学性。

Just as Jack has mastered English, so have his two sisters.
杰克掌握了英语，他的两个姐姐也是如此。

一些以 as if 和 as though 引导的状语从句可以充当表语。

It looks as if the dog is afraid of its master.
看起来仿佛这条狗很怕它的主人。

It seems as though spring is here already.
仿佛春天已经来了。

由 as if 或 as though 引导的方式状语从句也有虚拟语气的情况。

She behaves as if she were the boss of the company.
她表现得好像她是这家公司的老板一样。

He treats me as though I were a stranger to him.
他对待我就像陌生人一样。

由 as if 引导的表语从句也可能使用虚拟语气。

It seems as if the rain were a part of his plan.
似乎这场大雨是他计划的一部分。

The virtual image created by technology appears as if it were true.

这个科技制作出来的虚像看起来仿佛真的一样。

The wood feels as though it were fine wool.

这木头摸起来像是细绵羊毛一样。

在 as if 或 as though 引导的从句中用不用虚拟语气，还需要根据从句的含义来判断。

It looks as if it is going to rain.

看起来似乎要下雨了。

It sounds as though she is crying.

听起来好像她在哭。

8.8　比较状语从句

比较状语从句的常用引导词 than 需要和主句中的比较级形式（more, less 或其他形式）配合使用才构成比较关系（more... than... 结构）。

Jack is taller than I (am).

杰克比我高。

相对于主格 I，宾格 me 更多的是出现在非正式文体中。

Jack is taller than me.

杰克比我高。

比较状语从句中和主句里相同的成分通常可以省略。

China develops faster than Japan (does).

中国发展比日本快。

He is smarter than his brother (is).

他比他的兄弟更聪明。

This book is less expensive than that one (is).

这本书没有那本书贵。

Kate has less money than I (do).

凯特的钱比我的少。

Wheat plants require less water than rice plants (do).

小麦植物比大米植物需要的水少。

Kate has fewer friends than I (do).

凯特的朋友比我的少。

当句子里的可比较对象多于两个时，如果 than 后的成分省略，就有可能造成句子歧义。

He loves his dog more than his children.

上面这个句子可能有下面两种含义（为了便于理解，我们采用直译的方式）。

He loves his dog more than he loves his children.

他爱他的狗的程度超过了他爱他的孩子们的程度。

He loves his dog more than his children love his dog.

他爱他的狗的程度超过了他的孩子们爱他的狗的程度。

as... as... 结构表示等量比较，主句含有否定时还可以使用 so... as... 结构替代。

Jack is as tall as I am.

杰克和我一样高。

Roses are not as fragrant as violets are.

Roses are not so fragrant as violets are.

玫瑰不像紫罗兰那么香。

the more... the more... , the less... the less... , the more... the less... 和 the less... the more... 等结构也是常用的比较形式。

The harder you work, the better your English will be.

你越努力，你的英语就会越好。

The longer they work, the higher their pension will be.

他们工作时间越长，他们的养老金就越多。

The more time we spend with the professor, the more we like him.

和这位教授待的时间越久，我们越喜欢他。

The more Jack flatters me, the less I like him.

杰克越是奉承我，我越不喜欢他。

The more you take, the less you have.

你索取得越多，你拥有得越少。

The less we have, the more we want.

我们拥有得越少，我们想要得越多。

The fewer friends we make, the lonelier we will be.

我们交的朋友越少，我们越孤独。

The less resource we get from the nature, the less harm we cause to it.

我们向大自然索取资源越少，我们对它的伤害也就越小。

The fewer classes you miss, the less you are behind.

你越少缺课，越不会落后那么多。

8.9 让步状语从句

让步状语从句的常用引导词包括 although, though, even though, even if, while, as 等。

Although the city is a little old, it is still very interesting.

尽管这个城市有点老，但仍然很有意思。

Though she behaves properly, the boss doesn't like her.

尽管她表现得体，但老板还是不喜欢她。

I went out even though it was raining heavily.

尽管雨下得很大，但我还是出去了。

I will go out even if it rains tomorrow.

即使明天下雨，我也要出去。

While the salary is acceptable, the location of the company is not ideal.

尽管工资可以接受，但公司地点不理想。

从属连词 as 引导让步状语从句时，通常使用倒装结构。

Complicated as the tool is, it is extremely useful.

尽管这个工具复杂，但它非常有用。

Child as he is, he knows a lot.

尽管他还是个孩子，但他懂得很多。

Try as he might, he could not resolve it by himself.

他努力解决但自己还是解决不了。

Be that as it may, I really think you should go now.

尽管如此，我真的觉得你该走了。

由 wh- 词 +ever 构成的引导词、由 no matter+wh- 词构成的引导词，以及 whether...
or 等也可以引导让步状语从句。

I will continue my project whatever he may tell me.
无论他告诉我什么，我都会继续我的项目。

Whichever he prefers, I will insist on my choice.
不管他偏爱哪一个，我会坚持我的选择。

Stop doing this, whoever you are.
不管你是谁，停止做这件事。

The picture seems wrong, however you look at it.
无论你怎么看，这张图片似乎都有问题。

I will continue my project no matter what he may tell me.
无论他告诉我什么，我都会继续我的项目。

No matter whose job it is, we can take it over.
不管这是谁的工作，我们都可以接管过来。

Stay and wait for help, no matter where you are.
无论你在哪里，待在那里等待救援。

I am going to do this whether you like it or not.

我准备做这件事，不管你喜不喜欢。

知 识 应 用

选择题

1. We'll stay at home _____ it rains tomorrow.

    A. and   B. if   C. but   D. so

2. —Shall we go for a picnic in the forest park tomorrow?

    —Yes, _____ it rains heavily.

    A. if   B. unless   C. until   D. when

3. _____ you smile at others, they will smile back.

    A. Before   B. When   C. Until   D Though

4. Our world will get better and better _____ each of us lives a greener life.

    A. before   B. if   C. though   D. until

5. I didn't accept his help _____ I wanted to try it myself.

    A. because   B. though   C. until   D. unless

6. If you don't understand something, you may research, study, and talk to other people _____ you figure it out.

    A. because   B. though   C. until   D. since

7. _____ birds use their feathers for flight, some of their feathers are for other purposes.

    A. Once   B. If   C. Although   D. Because

8. _____ the damage is done, it will take many years for the farmland to recover.

    A. Until   B. Unless   C. Once   D. Although

9. The young couple, who returned my lost wallet, left _____ I could ask for their names.

    A. while   B. before   C. after   D. since

10. No sooner _____ stepped on the stage than the audience broke into thunderous applause.

    A. had Mo Yan   B. Mo Yan had   C. has Mo Yan   D. Mo Yan has

第 9 章

省略与强调

省略是将重复或多余的内容省去，使表达更为简洁高效。强调通过词汇或句法手段把主要信息凸显出来，达到强调的目的。

9.1 省略

省略现象非常繁杂，我们只把最常用的现象归纳出来（尤其是各种句子成分的省略现象），不求全面但求清晰实用。而且为了方便看出省略的部分，我们把省略的例句都附上还原版本。下面我们以清晰为原则进行分类展开。

1. 主语的省略

主语的省略通常出现在口语中。省略的主语通常是第一人称 I、第二人称 you（包括祈使句）和第三人称 he, she, they 或 it（有时需要通过上下文才能确定它的具体含义）等。

Sounds good.（省略后）
It sounds good.（省略前）
听起来不错。

Doesn’t matter.（省略后）
It doesn’t matter.（省略前）
没关系。

Hope so.（省略后）
I hope so.（省略前）
希望如此。

Don’t know anything about it.（省略后）
I don’t know anything about it.（省略前）

一点儿都不知道。

Want some?（省略后）
Do you want some?（省略前）
想要一些吗？

Open the door, please.（省略后）
You open the door, please.（省略前）
请开一下门。

Just wait there, will you?（省略后）
You just wait there, will you?（省略前）
就在那里等着好吗？

2. 谓语的省略

谓语（包括系动词）的省略一般出现在并列句中的第二个分句或从句里。

You do your work, and I mine.
You do your work, and I do mine.
你做你的工作，我（做）我的。

China develops faster than Japan.
China develops faster than Japan does.
China develops faster than Japan develops.
中国比日本发展快。

The little boy runs as fast as Jack.
The little boy runs as fast as Jack does.
The little boy runs as fast as Jack runs.
这个小男孩跑得和杰克一样快。

在口语中系动词有省略的现象：

You hungry?
Are you hungry?
饿吗？

3. 主语和谓语同时省略

主语和谓语（包括系动词）同时省略的现象主要出现在口语中，或者对疑问句的回答中。

Glad to see you again.

I am glad to see you again.

很高兴再次见到你。

Nice to meet you.

It is nice to meet you.

见到你很高兴。

What a day!

What a day it is!

多好（或者糟糕）的一天啊！

What are you staring at now?

A tall boy.

I am staring at a tall boy.

你在看什么？

一个高个子的男孩。

What are you writing?

A letter.

I am writing a letter.

你正在写什么？

一封信。

4. 宾语的省略

宾语（包括表语和介词宾语等）的省略也很常见，广泛存在于疑问句的答语（只保留系动词、情态动词，或借助助动词等），以及并列句和复合句中。

Do you love music?

Yes, I do.

Yes, I love music.

你喜欢音乐吗？

是的，我喜欢。

Are you a student?

Yes, I am.

Yes, I am a student.

你是学生吗？

是的，我是。

If you want to tell me the story, then tell me.

If you want to tell me the story, then tell me the story.

如果你想给我讲这个故事，那就给我讲。

Can you show me your picture?

Ok. Let me show you.

Let me show you my picture.

你能给我看看你的图片吗？

好的，我给你看。

There are huge amounts of garbage in and around the city.

There are huge amounts of garbage in the city and around the city.

在市里和市周围都有大量的垃圾。

We eat what we can.

We eat what we can eat.

我们吃我们能吃的。

They are excited, and we are, too.

They are excited, and we are excited, too.

他们很激动，我们也是。

I asked him whether he was elected as the committee member, but he told me he didn't know.

I asked him whether he was elected as the committee member, but he told me he didn't know whether he was elected as the committee member.

我问他是否当选为委员会成员了，他告诉我说他不知道。

5. 谓语和宾语同时省略

谓语和宾语同时省略，通常要保留情态动词或借助动词。

You want me to speak English, but I don't think I can.

You want me to speak English, but I don't think I can speak English.

你想让我说英语，但我觉得我不能。

If I can help you, then I will.

If I can help you, then I will help you.

如果我能帮你，我就会的。

I will help you if Jack does.

I will help you if Jack helps you.

如果杰克帮你，我就帮你。

Jack loves Mary more than I.

Jack loves Mary more than I do.

Jack loves Mary more than I love Mary.

杰克比我更爱玛丽。

6. 定状补的省略

Three of the girls went to the park, and the rest went to the zoo.

Three of the girls went to the park, and the rest of the girls went to the zoo.

这些女孩中的三个去了公园，其余的去了动物园。

I explain the first part of the story, and leave the second part to you.

I explain the first part of the story, and leave the second part of the story to you.

我来解释故事的第一部分，把第二部分留给你。

Everybody knows that you will do whatever I would love you to.

Everybody knows that you will do whatever I would love you to do.

大家都知道你会做任何我希望你做的。

I will do what you tell me to.

I will do what you tell me to do.

我会做你让我做的。

I will not go there unless I have to.

I will not go there unless I have to go there.

我是不会去那里的，除非不得不去。

I know that he must have done that, because I forced him to.

I know that he must have done that, because I forced him to do that.

我知道他一定做了那事，因为我强迫他了。

7. 其他常见省略

定语从句的关系代词在作宾语时的省略。

The book you bought for me was missing.

The book that you bought for me was missing.

The book which you bought for me was missing.
你给我买的那本书找不到了。

宾语从句或表语从句中的引导词 that 的省略。

I think you are right.
I think that you are right.
我认为你是对的。

All I want to say is I don't want to start now.
All I want to say is that I don't want to start now.
所有我想说的就是我不想现在就开始。

表虚拟语气的从句引导词 if 的省略（同时注意倒装结构）。

Were it not for your help, I would not have succeeded.
If it were not for your help, I would not have succeeded.
如果不是你的帮助，我不可能获得成功。

Should you have any questions, please feel free to contact us.
If you should have any questions, please feel free to contact us.
如果你有任何问题，请联系我们。

Had I known that, I would not have come here.
If I had known that, I would not have come here.
如果我知道那一点，我就不会来这里了。

还有一些特殊的引导词省略现象，如在先行词是 way 的定语从句中，引导词 that 或 in which 的省略等。

I like the way she talks.
I like the way that she talks.
I like the way in which she talks.
我喜欢她说话的方式。

由 when, whenever, while, once, though, as 等引导的状语从句中，主语和主句主语相同时的省略。

When walking in the street, I met Tom.
在街上散步的时候，我遇到了汤姆。
We can use it when dealing with business.

当处理生意时，我们可以用它。

When asked about his private life, the actor kept silent.

当被问道他的私生活时，这位演员保持了沉默。

Whenever talking to the professor, I feel inspired.

每当和这个教授谈话，我都倍受鼓舞。

He listened to his favorite songs while jogging.

他慢跑时听自己最喜欢的歌曲。

While detained by immigration authorities, we felt extremely helpless.

在被移民当局拘留期间，我们感觉极度无助。

Once benefiting from the policy, the local people will support it.

一旦从这项政策中获益，当地人就会支持它。

Once punished by failure, the activists will realize the defect of their project.

一旦受到失败的惩罚，这些激进分子就会意识到他们计划的缺陷。

Though submitted on time, the essay was not well written.

尽管被准时上交，但这篇文章写得不好。

Though knowing nothing about the area, she still went there alone.

尽管对这个地区一无所知，她还是独自一人去了那里。

Please fill the table with the data as instructed.

请按照指示用这些数据填表。

由 when, whenever, where 等引导的从句中，虚主语 it 和 be 动词的省略。

When possible, try to use the phrases that we have learned.

When it is possible, try to use the phrases that we have learned.

如果可能的话，试着使用我们学过的这些短语。

I will help you whenever necessary.

I will help you whenever it is necessary.

任何时候需要，我都会帮你的。

Please help me with the project if possible.

Please help me with the project if it is possible.

如果可能的话，请在这个项目上帮助我。

Check the details, and make changes where necessary.

Check the details, and make changes where it is necessary.

检查一下细节，在需要的地方做出改动。

从句为主系（be）表句型，并且和主句主语一致时的省略。

When in Rome, do as the Romans do.

When you are in Rome, you should do as the Romans do.

入乡随俗。

Although small, the apartment is cozy.

Although it is small, the apartment is cozy.

尽管这个公寓很小，但很温馨。

名词性从句也有这样的现象（wh-+to do），常见的有 where, what, whom, how, where 等。

I don't know what to do.

I don't know what I should do.

我不知道该做什么。

I don't know which to choose.

I don't know which I should choose.

我不知道该选哪一个。

I don't know whom to choose.

I don't know whom I should choose.

我不知道该选哪一位。

I don't know how to do it.

I don't know how I should do it.

我不知道该怎么做。

I don't know where to go.

I don't know where I should go.

我不知道去哪里。

9.2 ▶ 独立主格

省略还可能产生独立主格结构。一般是把复合句中的状语从句的相应成分进行省略，或者把并列句中的其中一个分句的相应成分进行省略。

当从句或并列句分句里系动词为 be 动词时，连词和 be 动词省略。下面的几组例子对比表明了省略的现象。

The girl ran to her parents, and her eyes were full of tears.（省略前）

The girl ran to her parents, her eyes full of tears.（省略后）

这个女孩跑向了她的父母，眼里满含泪水。

把从句或并列句分句里的谓语动词变为非谓语动词形式，并把连词省略。下面的几组例子对比表明了省略的现象。

If time permits, I will go there with you.（省略前）
Time permitting, I will go there with you.（省略后）
时间允许的话，我将会跟你去那里。

When the work was finished, we went home happily.（省略前）
The work finished, we went home happily.（省略后）
工作完成后，我们高兴地回家了。

We only draw an outline now, and the details can be worked out later.（省略前）
We only draw an outline now, the details to be worked out later.（省略后）
我们现在先列出大纲来，细节以后再磋商。

还有一类独立主格结构，常常以 with 开头。

The boy with a hat on is my brother.
那个戴着帽子的男孩是我的兄弟。
With production up by 10 percent, the company continued to dominate the market.
产量增长了百分之十，这个公司继续主导市场。
Don't talk with your mouth full of food.
不要在满嘴食物时说话。
With the world changing fast, we have to face something new every day.
随着世界的快速变化，我们每天都要面对新的事物。
You can't imagine how the actress finished the task with her feet wounded so much.
你无法想象这位女演员是怎么在脚伤这么重的情况下完成任务的。

9.3　强调

除了省略不重要的内容，强调也是一种突出重要内容的一种手段。强调的手法多种多样，此处仅把常用的强调方法列举一下。

9.3.1　通过词汇强调

I do love music.（加助动词强调）
我确实喜欢音乐。
I did help him when he was in need.（加助动词强调）

我确实在他需要的时候帮助了他。

Do be quiet when the boy is sleeping. (加助动词强调)

孩子睡觉的时候务必要安静。

I toured the whole city on the very first day. (加形容词强调)

在第一天我就参观了整个城市。

I practice my English every single day. (加形容词强调)

每一天我都练习英语。

I waited and waited. (通过重复强调)

我等啊等。

Where on earth are you hiding? (通过短语强调)

你究竟藏在哪里了?

The soup is just out of the world! (通过短语强调)

这汤美味极了。

I think the world of you. (通过短语强调)

我非常看重你。

His family is all the world to him. (通过短语强调)

他的家庭就是他的一切。

I don't like him at all. (通过短语强调)

我一点都不喜欢他。

I refer to none other than our friend from Charleston, Captain Rhett Butler. (通过短语强调)

我指的不是别人,正是我们来自查理斯顿的朋友瑞德·巴特勒船长。

9.3.2　通过句型强调

1. It is...that... 强调句型

It was English that helped Jane during the meeting.
是英语在会议中帮助了简。

It was at the party that Jane met her old friends.
简是在上周的聚会上遇到了她的老朋友们。

2. not...until... 强调句型

I did not go home until five o'clock.
我直到五点才回家。

Not until five o'clock did he arrive.
他直到五点才到达。

3. 前移和后移

Fame and fortune I don't want.

名声和财富我不想要。

This I believe.

这一点我相信。

It is no use crying over spilt milk.

为打翻的牛奶哭泣是没有用的。

4. 倒装

He is tired, and so am I.

你很累，我也是。

He felt nervous, and so did Jane.

他感到很紧张，简也是。

Extremely hungry was the homeless child.

这个无家可归的孩子极度饥饿。

Only by practice can we learn English well.

只有通过练习我们才能把英语学好。

Little did I know about the country.

我对这个国家知之甚少。

Not a single person had I met in that region.

我在那个地区一个人都没见到。

知 识 应 用

请识别下列句子中的独立主格或强调部分。

1. I couldn't do my homework with that noise going on.

2. Bats are surprisingly long-lived creatures, some having a life span of around 20 years.

3. The old couple often take a walk after supper in the park with their pet dog following.

4. I send you 100 dollars today, the rest to follow in a year.

5. Much time spent sitting at a desk, office workers are generally troubled by health problems.

6. Not until recently did they encourage the development of tourist-related activities in the rural areas.

7. Only by practice can we learn English well.

8. Only when Lily walked into the office did she realize that she had left the contract at home.

9. It was not until he came back from Africa that he met the girl he would like to marry.

10. It is what you do rather than what you say that matters.

综 合 实 践

　　本章是综合实践。语法知识是为理解和应用语言而服务的，所以要在实践中检验所学。单独的句子有时会因为没有语境而难以理解，甚至产生歧义，所以本章直接选取几篇考试真题中的文章，对其中的重点句型进行分析。

10.1　高考英语真题句式

　　请指出下面画线部分的句子分别属于哪一种句子类型（简单句、并列句或复合句）。如果含有从句，请指出从句类型。

Life in the Clear

　　(1) Transparent animals let light pass through their bodies the same way light passes through a window. These animals typically live between the surface of the ocean and a depth of about 3,300 feet—as far as most light can reach. Most of them are extremely delicate and can be damaged by a simple touch. Sonke Johnsen, a scientist in biology, says, "These animals live through their life alone. They never touch anything unless they're eating it, or unless something is eating them."

　　And they are as clear as glass. How does an animal become see-through? It's trickier than you might think.

　　The objects around you are visible because they interact with light. Light typically travels in a straight line. But some materials slow and scatter light, bouncing it away from its original path. Others absorb light, stopping it dead in its tracks. (2) Both scattering and absorption make an object look different from other objects around it, so you can see it easily.

　　But a transparent object doesn't absorb or scatter light, at least not very much. Light can pass through it without bending or stopping. (3) That means a transparent object doesn't look very different from the surrounding air or water. You don't see it—you see the things behind it.

　　To become transparent, an animal needs to keep its body from absorbing or scattering light. (4) Living materials can stop light because they contain pigments that absorb specific colors of light. But a transparent animal doesn't have pigments, so its tissues won't absorb light. According to Johnsen, avoiding absorption is actually easy. The real challenge is preventing light from scattering.

Animals are built of many different materials—skin, fat, and more—and light moves through each at a different speed. (5) Every time light moves into a material with a new speed, it bends and scatters. Transparent animals use different tricks to fight scattering. Some animals are simply very small or extremely flat. Without much tissue to scatter light, it is easier to be see-through. Others build a large, clear mass of non-living jelly-like material and spread themselves over it.

Larger transparent animals have the biggest challenge, because they have to make all the different tissues in their bodies slow down light exactly as much as water does. They need to look uniform. But how they're doing it is still unknown. One thing is clear: for these larger animals, staying transparent is an active process. When they die, they turn a non-transparent milky white.（2015 年高考英语北京卷）

10.2　大学英语四级考试真题句式

请指出下面画线部分的句子分别属于哪一种句子类型（简单句、并列句或复合句）。如果含有从句，请指出从句类型。

Popping food into the microwave for a couple of minutes may seem utterly harmless, but Europe's stock of these quick-cooking ovens emit as much carbon as nearly 7 million cars, a new study has found. And the problem is growing. With costs falling and kitchen appliances becoming "status" items, owners are throwing away microwaves after an average of eight years. (6) This is pushing sales of new microwaves which are expected to reach 135 million annually in the EU by the end of the decade.

A study by the University of Manchester calculated the emissions of CO_2—the main greenhouse gas responsible for climate change—at every stage of microwaves, from manufacture to waste disposal. "It is electricity consumption by microwaves that has the biggest impact on the environment," say the authors. (7) The authors also calculate that the emissions from using 19 microwaves over a year are the same as those from using a car. According to the same study, efforts to reduce consumption should focus on improving consumer awareness and behavior. For example, consumers could use appliances in a more efficient way by adjusting the time of cooking to the type of food.

(8) However, David Reay, professor of carbon management, argues that, although microwaves use a great deal of energy, their emissions are minor compared to those from cars. In the UK alone, there are around 30 million cars. These cars emit more than all the microwaves in the EU. (9) Backing this up, recent data show that passenger cars in the UK

emitted 69 million tons of CO_2 in 2015. This is 10 times the amount this new microwave oven study estimates for annual emissions for all the microwave ovens in the EU. Further, the energy used by microwaves is lower than any other form of cooking. (10) <u>Among common kitchen appliances used for cooking, microwaves are the most energy efficient, followed by a stove and finally a standard oven.</u> Thus, rising microwave sales could be seen as a positive thing.（2019 年 12 月大学英语四级考试真题 Part Ⅲ Section C Passage Two）

10.3 大学英语六级考试真题句式

请指出下面画线部分的句子分别属于哪一种句子类型（简单句、并列句或复合句）。如果含有从句，请指出从句类型。

When the right person is holding the right job at the right moment, that person's influence is greatly expanded. (11) <u>That is the position in which Janet Yellen, who is expected to be confirmed as the next chair of the Federal Reserve Band (Fed) in January, now finds herself.</u> If you believe, as many do, that unemployment is the major economic and social concern of our day, then it is no stretch to think Yellen is the powerful person in the world right now.

(12) <u>Throughout the 2008 financial crisis and the recession and recovery that followed, central banks have taken on the role of stimulators of last resort, holding up the global economy with vast amounts of money in the form of asset buying.</u> Yellen, previously a Fed vice chair, was one of the principal architects of the Fed's $3.8 trillion money dump. (13) <u>A star economist known for her groundbreaking work on labor markets, Yellen was a kind of prophetess early on in the crisis for her warnings about the subprime meltdown.</u> Now it will be her job to get the Fed and the markets out of the biggest and most unconventional monetary program in history without derailing the fragile recovery.

The good news is that Yellen, 67, is particularly well suited to meet these challenges. (14) <u>She has a keen understanding of financial markets, an appreciation for their imperfections and a strong belief that human suffering is more related to unemployment than anything else.</u>

Some experts worry that Yellen will be inclined to chase unemployment to the neglect of inflation. (15) <u>But with wages still relatively flat and the economy increasingly divided between the well-off and the long-term unemployed, more people worry about the opposite, deflation that would aggravate the economy's problems.</u>

Either way, the incoming Fed chief will have to walk a fine line in slowly ending the stimulus. It must be steady enough to deflate bubbles and bring markets back down to earth but not so quick that it creates another credit crisis.

Unlike many past Fed leaders, Yellen is not one to buy into the finance industry's argument that it should be left alone to regulate itself. She knows all along the Fed has been too slack on regulation of finance.

Yellen is likes to address the issue right after she pushes unemployment below 6%, stabilizes markets and makes sure that the recovery is more inclusive and robust. As Princeton Professor Alan Blinder says, "She's smart as a whip, deeply logical, willing to argue but also a good listener. She can persuade without creating hostility." All those traits will be useful as the global economy's new power player takes on its most annoying problems.(《全国大学英语四、六级考试大纲（2016 年修订版）》)

10.4　考研英语（一）真题句式

请指出下面画线部分的句子分别属于哪一种句子类型（简单句、并列句或复合句）。如果含有从句，请指出从句类型。

(16) One basic weakness in a conservation system based wholly on economic motives is that most members of the land community have no economic value. Yet these creatures are members of the biotic community and, if its stability depends on its integrity, they are entitled to continuance.

When one of these noneconomic categories is threatened and, if we happen to love it, we invent excuses to give it economic importance. At the beginning of the century songbirds were supposed to be disappearing. (17) Scientists jumped to the rescue with some distinctly shaky evidence to the effect that insects would eat us up if birds failed to control them. The evidence had to be economic in order to be valid.

It is painful to read these roundabout accounts today. (18) We have no land ethic yet, but we have at least drawn nearer the point of admitting that birds should continue as a matter of intrinsic right, regardless of the presence or absence of economic advantage to us.

A parallel situation exists in respect of predatory mammals and fish-eating birds. Time was when biologists somewhat overworked the evidence that these creatures preserve the health of game by killing the physically weak, or that they prey only on "worthless" species. Here again, the evidence had to be economic in order to be valid. It is only in recent years that we hear the more honest argument that predators are members of the community, and that no special interest has the right to exterminate them for the sake of a benefit, real or fancied, to itself.

Some species of trees have been "read out of the party" by economics-minded foresters because they grow too slowly, or have too low a sale value to pay as timber crops. (19) In Europe, where forestry is ecologically more advanced, the noncommercial tree species are recognized as members of the native forest community, to be preserved as such, within reason. Moreover, some have been found to have a valuable function in building up soil fertility. The interdependence of the forest and its constituent tree species, ground flora, and fauna is taken for granted.

To sum up: a system of conservation based solely on economic self-interest is hopelessly lopsided. (20) It tends to ignore, and thus eventually to eliminate, many elements in the land community that lack commercial value, but that are essential to its healthy functioning. It assumes, falsely, that the economic parts of the biotic clock will function without the uneconomic parts.（2010 年考研英语（一）真题 Section Ⅱ Part C）

10.5 考研英语（二）真题句式

请指出下面画线部分的句子分别属于哪一种句子类型（简单句、并列句或复合句）。如果含有从句，请指出从句类型。

Biologists estimate that as many as 2 million lesser prairie chickens—a kind of bird living on stretching grasslands—once lent red to the often grey landscape of the midwestern and southwestern United States. But just some 22,000 birds remain today, occupying about 16% of the species' historic range.

(21) The crash was a major reason the U.S. Fish and Wildlife Service (USFWS) decided to formally list the bird as threatened. "The lesser prairie chicken is in a desperate situation," said USFWS Director Daniel Ashe. Some environmentalists, however, were disappointed. (22) They had pushed the agency to designate the bird as "endangered", a status that gives federal officials greater regulatory power to crack down on threats. But Ashe and others argued that the "threatened" tag gave the federal government flexibility to try out new, potentially less confrontational conservations approaches. (23) In particular, they called for forging closer collaborations with western state governments, which are often uneasy with federal action, and with the private landowners who control an estimated 95% of the prairie chicken's habitat.

Under the plan, for example, the agency said it would not prosecute landowners or businesses that unintentionally kill, harm, or disturb the bird, as long as they had signed a rang-wide management plan to restore prairie chicken habitat. (24) Negotiated by USFWS and the states, the plan requires individuals and businesses that damage habitat as part of their operations to pay into a fund to replace every acre destroyed with 2 new acres of suitable habitat. The fund will also be used to compensate landowners who set aside habitat. USFWS also set an interim goal of restoring prairie chicken populations to an annual average of 67,000 birds over the next 10 years. (25) And it gives the Western Association of Fish and Wildlife Agencies (WAFWA), a coalition of state agencies, the job of monitoring progress. Overall, the idea is to let "states remain in the driver's seat for managing the species," Ashe said.

Not everyone buys the win-win rhetoric. Some Congress members are trying to block the plan, and at least a dozen industry groups, four states, and three environmental groups are challenging it in federal court. Not surprisingly, industry groups and states generally argue it goes too far, environmentalists say it doesn't go far enough. "The federal government is giving responsibility for managing the bird to the same industries that are pushing it to extinction," says biologist Jay Lininger.（2016 年考研英语（二）真题 Section Ⅱ Part A Text 2）

附录 1　知识应用部分答案

第 1 章

1. 主＋谓＋宾
2. 主＋系＋表
3. 主＋谓＋宾
4. 主＋谓
5. 主＋谓＋宾
6. 主＋谓＋宾
7. 主＋系＋表
8. 主＋谓＋宾
9. 主＋谓＋宾
10. 主＋谓＋宾＋宾补

第 2 章

1. 名词 humans 充当主语；名词 plastic 充当宾语。
2. 动词短语 winds up 充当谓语。
3. 形容词 effective 充当定语，修饰 way。
4. 介词短语 of the greater wax moth 充当定语，修饰 the worms。
5. 动名词 shopping 充当定语，修饰 bag。
6. 动名词 chewing 充当主语。
7. 名词 findings 充当主语。
8. 不定式短语 to break down their everyday food 充当定语，修饰 the worms' ability。
9. 不定式短语 to break this bond 充当定语，修饰 a method or system。

10. 不定式短语 to identify the cause of the breakdown 充当表语。

第 3 章

1. C
2. C
3. C
4. D
5. C
6. C
7. A
8. D
9. B
10. B

第 4 章

一、

1. C
2. C
3. D
4. B
5. A
6. B
7. D

二、

1. Does the new product consist of four main parts inside?
2. Whose advice did Susan follow to design smart shoes?

3. What an excellent Chinese basketball
player Yao Ming is!

第 5 章

（1）复合句
（2）简单句
（3）复合句
（4）简单句
（5）复合句
（6）复合句
（7）复合句
（8）简单句
（9）简单句
（10）简单句
（11）简单句
（12）简单句
（13）简单句
（14）复合句
（15）简单句
（16）简单句（破折号后为并列句）
（17）复合句
（18）复合句
（19）简单句
（20）复合句
（21）简单句
（22）简单句
（23）简单句
（24）复合句
（25）简单句
（26）简单句
（27）简单句
（28）简单句
（29）简单句
（30）简单句
（31）复合句
（32）复合句
（33）简单句
（34）复合句

第 6 章

1. A
2. D
3. B
4. B
5. C
6. C
7. B
8. A
9. C
10. B

第 7 章

1. D
2. C
3. B
4. A
5. A
6. C
7. D
8. B
9. C
10. B

第 8 章

1. B
2. B
3. B
4. B
5. A
6. C
7. C
8. C
9. B
10. A

第　9　章

1. with that noise going on 为独立主格部分。

2. some having a life span of around 20 years 为独立主格部分。

3. with their pet dog following 为独立主格部分。

4. the rest to follow in a year 为独立主格部分。

5. much time spent sitting at a desk 为独立主格部分。

6. recently 为强调部分。

7. by practice 为强调部分。

8. when Lily walked into the office 为强调部分。

9. he came back from Africa 为强调部分。

10. what you do 为强调部分。

第　10　章

（1）复合句。含有一个省略引导词的定语从句。

（2）并列句。

（3）复合句。含有一个省略引导词的宾语从句。

（4）复合句。含有一个 because 引导的原因状语从句，以及一个 that 引导的定语从句。

（5）复合句。含有一个 every time 引导的时间状语从句。

（6）复合句。含有一个 which 引导的定语从句。

（7）复合句。含有一个 that 引导的宾语从句。

（8）复合句。含有一个 that 引导的宾语从句，以及一个 although 引导的让步状语从句。

（9）复合句。含有一个 that 引导的宾语从句。

（10）简单句。

（11）复合句。含有两个定语从句，分别是 in which 引导的定语从句和 who 引导的定语从句。

（12）复合句。含有一个由 that 引导的定语从句。

（13）简单句。

（14）复合句。含有一个 that 引导的同位语从句。

（15）复合句。含有一个由 that 引导的定语从句。

（16）复合句。含有一个由 that 引导的表语从句。

（17）复合句。含有一个由 that 引导的同位语从句，以及一个由 if 引导的条件状语从句。

（18）并列句。but 后的分句含有一个由 that 引导的宾语从句。

（19）复合句。含有一个由 where 引导的定语从句。

（20）复合句。含有两个由 that 引导的定语从句。

（21）复合句。含有一个省略引导词的定语从句。

（22）复合句。含有一个 that 引导的定语从句。

（23）复合句。含有两个定语从句，分别由 which 和 who 引导。

（24）复合句。含有一个 that 引导的定语从句。

（25）简单句。

附录 2 不规则动词表

按照本书的定位，不规则动词表仅展示常见变化规则（见附表 2-1 ～附表 2-8）。

附表 2-1 不规则动词表 1

序 号	动词原形	过去式	过去分词	备 注
1	awake	awoke	awoken	也有 awaked 的现象
2	arise	arose	arisen	
3	be	was, were	been	was 是 is 和 am 的过去式；were 是 are 的过去式
4	bear	bore	born, borne	表出生时用 born
5	beat	beat	beaten	
6	become	became	become	
7	begin	began	begun	
8	bend	bent	bent	
9	bet	bet, betted	bet, betted	
10	bind	bound	bound	
11	bite	bit	bitten	
12	bleed	bled	bled	
13	blow	blew	blown	
14	break	broke	broken	
15	breed	bred	bred	
16	bring	brought	brought	
17	broadcast	broadcast	broadcast	
18	build	built	built	
19	burn	burned, burnt	burned, burnt	
20	burst	burst	burst	

附表 2-2　不规则动词表 2

序　号	动词原形	过去式	过去分词	备　注
1	buy	bought	bought	
2	cast	cast	cast	
3	catch	caught	caught	
4	choose	chose	chosen	
5	cling	clung	clung	
6	come	came	come	
7	cost	cost	cost	
8	creep	crept	crept	
9	cut	cut	cut	
10	deal	dealt	dealt	
11	dig	dug	dug	
12	dive	dived, dove	dived	
13	do	did	done	
14	draw	drew	drawn	
15	dream	dreamed, dreamt	dreamed, dreamt	
16	drink	drank	drunk	
17	drive	drove	driven	
18	dwell	dwelt, dwelled	dwelt, dwelled	
19	eat	ate	eaten	
20	fall	fell	fallen	

附表 2-3　不规则动词表 3

序　号	动词原形	过去式	过去分词	备　注
1	feed	fed	fed	
2	feel	felt	felt	
3	fight	fought	fought	
4	find	found	found	
5	fit	fitted, fit	fitted, fit	
6	flee	fled	fled	
7	fling	flung	flung	
8	fly	flew	flown	
9	forbid	forbade, forbad	forbidden	

续表

序　号	动词原形	过去式	过去分词	备　注
10	forget	forgot	forgotten	
11	forgive	forgave	forgiven	
12	freeze	froze	frozen	
13	get	got	got, gotten	
14	give	gave	given	
15	go	went	gone	
16	grow	grew	grown	
17	hang	hung	hung	作"处以绞刑"含义时属于规则变化
18	have	had	had	
19	hear	heard	heard	
20	hide	hid	hidden	

附表 2-4　不规则动词表 4

序　号	动词原形	过去式	过去分词	备　注
1	hit	hit	hit	
2	hold	held	held	
3	hurt	hurt	hurt	
4	keep	kept	kept	
5	knit	knitted, knit	knitted, knit	
6	know	knew	known	
7	lay	laid	laid	
8	lead	led	led	
9	lean	leaned, leant	leaned, leant	
10	leap	leaped, leapt	leaped, leapt	
11	learn	learned, learnt	learned, learnt	
12	leave	left	left	
13	lend	lent	lent	
14	let	let	let	

序　号	动词原形	过去式	过去分词	备　注
15	lie	lay	lain	lie 作"说谎"含义时属于规则变化
16	light	lighted, lit	lighted, lit	
17	lose	lost	lost	
18	make	made	made	
19	mean	meant	meant	
20	meet	met	met	

附表 2-5　不规则动词表 5

序　号	动词原形	过去式	过去分词	备　注
1	mistake	mistook	mistaken	
2	mow	mowed	mown, mowed	
3	pay	paid	paid	
4	plead	pled, pleaded	pled, pleaded	
5	prove	proved	proved, proven	
6	put	put	put	
7	quit	quit, quitted	quit, quitted	
8	read	read	read	过去式和过去分词读音为 [red]
9	rend	rent	rent	
10	ride	rode	ridden	
11	ring	rang	rung	ring 作"包围"含义时属于规则变化
12	rise	rose	risen	
13	run	ran	run	
14	say	said	said	
15	see	saw	seen	
16	seek	sought	sought	
17	sell	sold	sold	
18	send	sent	sent	
19	set	set	set	
20	sew	sewed	sewed, sewn	

附表 2-6　不规则动词表 6

序　号	动词原形	过去式	过去分词	备　注
1	shake	shook	shaken	
2	shave	shaved	shaved, shaven	
3	shed	shed	shed	
4	shine	shone, shined	shone, shined	
5	shoot	shot	shot	
6	show	showed	shown, showed	
7	shred	shredded, shred	shredded, shred	
8	shrink	shrank	shrunk	
9	shut	shut	shut	
10	sing	sang	sung	
11	sink	sank	sunk	
12	sit	sat	sat	
13	sleep	slept	slept	
14	slide	slid	slid	
15	smell	smelt, smelled	smelt, smelled	
16	speak	spoke	spoken	
17	speed	sped, speeded	sped, speeded	
18	spell	spelt, spelled	spelt, spelled	
19	spend	spent	spent	
20	spill	spilt, spilled	spilt, spilled	

附表 2-7　不规则动词表 7

序　号	动词原形	过去式	过去分词	备　注
1	spin	spun	spun	
2	spit	spat, spit	spat, spit	
3	split	split	split	
4	spoil	spoilt, spoiled	spoilt, spoiled	
5	spread	spread	spread	
6	spring	sprang, sprung	sprung	
7	stand	stood	stood	
8	steal	stole	stolen	
9	stick	stuck	stuck	
10	sting	stung	stung	

续表

序　号	动词原形	过去式	过去分词	备　注
11	strike	struck	struck	
12	string	strung	strung	
13	strive	strove, strived	striven, strived	
14	swear	swore	sworn	
15	sweat	sweat, sweated	sweat, sweated	
16	sweep	swept	swept	
17	swell	swelled	swollen, swelled	
18	swim	swam	swum	
19	swing	swung	swung	
20	take	took	taken	

附表 2-8　不规则动词表 8

序　号	动词原形	过去式	过去分词	备　注
1	teach	taught	taught	
2	tear	tore	torn	
3	tell	told	told	
4	think	thought	thought	
5	thrive	thrived, throve	thrived, thriven	
6	throw	threw	thrown	
7	tread	trod	trodden, trod	
8	upset	upset	upset	
9	wake	woke	woken	
10	wear	wore	worn	
11	weave	wove	woven	
12	wed	wedded, wed	wedded, wed	
13	weep	wept	wept	
14	wet	wetted, wet	wetted, wet	
15	win	won	won	
16	wind	wound	wound	wind 作"使透不过气"含义时属于规则变化
17	withdraw	withdrew	withdrawn	
18	wring	wrung	wrung	
19	write	wrote	written	